	DATE DUE		
2/4			
4/10/21			

GRACE & GLORY

Sally Gunnel of Great Britain at the
1992 Olympic Games in Barcelona.

GRACE & GLORY

A CENTURY OF WOMEN IN THE OLYMPICS

MULTI-MEDIA PARTNERS LTD.
WASHINGTON, D.C.

TRIUMPH BOOKS
CHICAGO

Produced and distributed by Triumph Books.

This book is available in quantity at special
discounts for your group or organization.
For further information, contact:

    Triumph Books
    644 South Clark Street
    Chicago, Illinois 60605
    (312) 939-3330

Printed in Canada.
ISBN 1-57243-116-4

Written by
Jane Leder

Editing
Siobhan Drummond and Elizabeth Rathburn

Editorial Assistance
Sarah Burgundy

Book design and typesetting
Joan Sommers Design

Cover design
Eileen Engel

CONTENTS

FOREWORD

by Joan Benoit Samuelson

Grace & Glory probably would not have been written if it hadn't been for the sweat and sacrifices of women athletes who were brave and daring enough to enter into the athletic arena—which has historically been dominated by men.

This book is a wonderful tribute to women who made great inroads and advancements in sports. Their stories have given countless women the confidence and inspiration to break down barriers in all areas of life—home, workplace, and playing fields. Through hard work, determination, drive and dedication, many of the women athletes in this book overcame disadvantaged backgrounds, social constraints, minimal opportunities, and other hardships to lead by stellar performances. In many cases, they won Olympic gold.

As a young female athlete, I was told that I couldn't run distances longer than a mile in competition. It was a common misconception then that women would do themselves bodily harm, thereby jeopardizing their ability to bear children, if they ran long distances.

In 1976, when I started to show promise as a distance runner, the longest Olympic competition was the 1,500-meter run. Who would have ever thought that the marathon would become an Olympic event in less than a decade? Without the perseverance, the secret entries in marathons, and the vocal demands of the women who came before me in my sport, I never would have had the opportunity to participate in the Olympic marathon in 1984. I think women athletes in all sports are similarly grateful to the pioneers among them.

The stories of athletic achievement among women are many, despite the opportunities for athletic success being few. The women who led the charge in their respective sports have served as role models for all of us who have followed in their footsteps.

With grace and glory, the women of this book have inspired many of us to run mile after mile in pursuit of excellence and fulfillment.

INTRODUCTION

Every four years for a century now, the modern-day Olympic Games have focused the world's attention on the healthy spirit of athletic competition. Superb athletes from many countries, all of which have seen enormous changes in the past one hundred years, proudly represent their people and celebrate their sports.

For Olympic women, the celebration now is particularly sweet. Their desire for respect as athletes and full participation in the Games has been all but fulfilled. Olympic women in the first half of the century often faced social and cultural mores that discouraged, even prohibited, their participation, but they paved the way for today's women athletes to compete fully in the Olympic Games.

Women were barred completely from the first modern-day Olympics held in Athens, Greece, in 1896. Four years later, in 1900 in Paris, France, they were allowed to compete, but the only sports open to them were golf, tennis, and yachting. Female athletes of the times were expected to be frail and modest; they were not supposed to sweat. Women athletes were accepted up to a point, but only as long as they remained "ladylike."

The turn of the century on the heels of the industrial revolution brought rapid change. Women gained the right to vote, shed their corsets for shorter skirts, and bobbed their hair. Technology and war brought them out of the home and into the workforce. The emphasis on "appropriate" sports gave way slowly. Women performed in demonstrations or exhibitions of sports such as swimming and gymnastics, thus gradually breaking down the public bias against their participation. For the first time, a few women became sports heroes.

As the decades passed, Olympic women came to symbolize society's changing views about women as athletes and about women in general. As athletes, they became stronger and more muscular. They trained hard, held up under pressure, and showed their emotions freely in victory and in defeat. Many women juggled Olympic training and competition with responsibilities as students, professionals, wives, and mothers. Many helped break down barriers of race, religion, and culture around the world. They won medals and hearts.

By 1984, television coverage of women's events in the Olympics was comparable to men's.

By 1988, more than a quarter of the athletes in the Olympics were women, and they participated in a growing number of sports. Four years later, more than 3,000 women competed. In these numbers, women athletes offered a wide range of personal styles. As role models to the millions of women watching, they demonstrated that being "ladylike" was no longer the only definition of what a woman ought to be.

Sports have been an important and increasingly visible means of changing the roles of women and documenting their progress in the world. From their entry into the Olympics in 1900 to the present, women in Olympic competition have held the attention of the world with their strength, courage, and grace.

ONE

The Sargent girls play soccer, 1900.

Excluded

SPORTS IN THE ANCIENT WORLD

Ancient Times TO 1896 Athletic training and competition played a central role in ancient Greece and in ancient Egypt. It is from the decorations on pottery and buildings, and from sculture and artifacts that we can piece together the world of women's sports in the distant past. Fifth-century vases document an athletic ritual for the girls of Attica at the Temple of Artemis. Other games for young women were held at Sparta and at Cyrene. In ancient Egypt, acrobatics and dance were considered sports for women. Shards and grave carvings from the ancient tombs show girls doing complicated acrobatic exercises.

The Greeks believed that mind and body could not be separated. In youth, girls as well as boys were required to train physically and to compete in athletic contests. For girls, however, fitness and courage were prized not for grace and glory but as an indication they could bear hardy sons. In Sparta, girls were instructed in wrestling, running, and throwing the quoit and the dart. The goal was to build healthier bodies that could withstand the pains of childbirth. But as adults, women were denied access to gymnasia and stadia and discouraged from public displays of athletic prowess. Their primary roles were wife and mother, and their strengths were directed toward ceremony and religion.

The most significant athletic competition for women in the ancient world

Small bronze of a Spartan girl runner

were the Games of Hera. They were held every four years to honor the Greek goddess who ruled over women and the earth. Married women did not compete, but young, adolescent, and unmarried women competed in age groups. They raced barefoot or in sandals, with their hair hanging down, dressed in short loose garments called chitons which bared their right shoulder and breast. The winners were crowned with olive branches and given a share of the cow sacrificed to the goddess.

The records of the ancient Olympics go back to 776 B.C. They began with a single 170-meter race. The race was a religious rite intended to inspire man with a divine heroic model. Women were barred from competing. As the Games expanded, women participated indirectly by entering their horses and chariots in the chariot race. The Spartan princess Kyniska might be said to have been the first female Olympian—her horses won the chariot race in 396 B.C., but she was not allowed to be present to collect her prize. In the second century A.D., the historian Pausanias wrote that "virgins were not refused admission (to the Olympics) as spectators," but married women were not admitted on pain of death. The ancient Olympics continued for nearly 1,200 years, until they were banned toward the end of the fourth century A.D. Women were excluded to the end.

ATALANTA

Greek Goddess of the Hunt

The ancient Greek goddesses of mythology were athletic and powerful. Tales of Atalanta, Athena, Artemis, and the warlike Amazons were popular. Of Atalanta it was said that she "loved adventure as much as the most dauntless hero and could outshoot, outrun and outwrestle" the men of one of the great ages of heroism.

The tales of Atalanta have come down with several variations. In one, she is a descendent of Prometheus, born to a father who had wanted a son. Deeply disappointed, he left her on a mountainside, where she was nurtured by a she-bear and raised by hunters. She was said to be as beautiful as she was strong and swift. She went into the world looking for adventure. Meleager, smitten by her beauty and impressed with her prowess, invited her to join the Calydonian boar hunt. She drew first blood, and when the boar finally fell, Meleager awarded her the hide, for which he lost his life. She sailed with Jason on the Argo in search of the golden fleece and participated in the funeral games for his uncle, where she wrestled the great hero Peleus and won. Eventually she returned to her family, who gave her a home but did not approve of her wild and unconventional ways. She was pressed to marry, which she was reluctant to do. She agreed at last to marry the suitor who could beat her in a footrace. Many tried, but all failed, and some said that they were killed as a result. It was Hippomenes who thought to enlist the help of Aphrodite, and she gave him three irresistible golden apples from the Garden of the Hesperides. He tossed them in Atalanta's path as they raced and thus was able to defeat her. She married Hippomenes and bore a son.

Etruscan vase with women runners.

THE FIRST MODERN OLYMPIC GAMES

The nineteenth century opened in the spirit of the romantic movement and closed as "an epoch of invention and progress." Exhibitions of all kinds were hugely popular, which may have been what inspired de Coubertin and his colleagues to revive the Olympics in 1896. There were no women allowed.

In Europe and America, women participated in sports considered ladylike—tennis, croquet, cycling, ice skating, and golf. Aristocratic women enjoyed equestrian sports and yachting. But participation in more physically strenuous sports—hockey, cricket, swimming, athletics—was not publicly accepted. Many modern sports developed at this time, but team sports, especially, tended to be segregated by gender. Women leaned toward individual sports, and such activity was often viewed as an aspect of courtship rather than competition. Prevailing attitudes about childbearing, quite the opposite of the ancients, discouraged excessive physical activity and thus restricted sports for many women.

Progress toward equality in sports, and in society generally, moved ahead slowly but steadily.

Encouraged by the suffragist movement, women began to work for greater independence, temperance reform, the right to vote, and protective legislation for themselves and for children. Technological advances reduced the burden of domestic chores shouldered by women. With more free time, many women joined the workforce. In France, Marie Curie discovered radium and eventually received two Nobel Prizes. Great Britain's Florence Nightingale founded modern nursing and worked tirelessly to care for the sick and wounded. In the U.S., Susan B. Anthony agitated for equal pay for women teachers, for coeducation, and for college training for young women. Women were first granted the right to vote in New Zealand in 1893, in Australia in 1902, and in Norway in 1907.

The American women's tennis team in 1895.

MELPOMENE

Running on the Margins

When the first modern Olympic Games were held in Athens in 1896, one woman, Melpomene, petitioned to compete in the marathon. She was denied entry. Against the wishes of her family and the Olympic organizers, Melpomene unofficially ran the forty kilometers from Marathon to Athens.

The race started midafternoon on the fifth day of the Games. Two dozen long-distance runners from five countries gathered on the bridge in Marathon, Greece. Their assistants, on bicycles, carried water, wine, brandy, and other magic potions to restore their charges. Melpomene readied herself for the race out of sight of the officials and ran parallel to the men until the official starter could no longer see her.

Led by French runner, Lermusiaux, the contenders ran through the hot, dusty countryside. As they weakened, they stopped to refresh themselves with glasses of wine and alcohol rubdowns. Some dropped out exhausted. Melpomene lost sight of the men but kept a steady pace. Onlookers gave her strange looks and taunted her along the way. She stopped for ten minutes in Pikermi, drank a glass of water, and continued the race. She passed exhausted runners lying in the shade who looked up in amazement.

As the Greek champion, Spiridon Louis, ran the last few steps of the race, spectators threw flowers, hats, jewelry, and money in his path. He had finished in 2 hours, 58 minutes, 50 seconds. Late that afternoon, Melpomene arrived at the stadium. She was not allowed to enter. There were no spectators and no cheers. She ran the final lap outside the stadium and finished in 4 hours, 30 minutes.

The oldest evidence of sport comes from ancient Egypt where sporting tradition goes back to the pharaohs nearly 3,000 years ago. Sports were one way Egyptian monarchs presented themselves to their people. The pharaoh was considered to have the actual physical strength of a warrior and hunter, as well as an athlete. However, the pharaoh's superiority was never questioned, and they did not compete in sports personally. The members of the royal house and private citizens competed during the "Jubilee," a festival that included athletics, combat, and water sport, along with noncompetitive games and activities such as dancing and hunting.

April 1896 Melpomene runs the marathon unofficially at the first modern Olympic Games in Athens May—October 1900 Nineteen women debut at the Olympic Games at the Universal Exposition in Paris January 1901 Queen Victoria dies September 1903 The Wright Brothers fly the first plane in Kitty Hawk, North Carolina December 1903 The Curies win the Nobel Prize in physics August—September 1904 Archery is introduced for women at the St. Louis Olympics 1906 Finland gives women the right to vote August—September 1906 Danish women demonstrate gymnastics at the Intercalated Olympics in Athens 1908 Ford sells the first automobile August—September 1908 Madge Syers of Great Britain wins the first figure skating gold medal at the London Olympics 1910 Annette Kellerman shocks the world when she swims Boston Harbor in an "indecent" bathing suit 1912 Harriet Quimby flies over the English Channel February 1912 Femina Sport, an exclusive sports club for women, is founded in France August—September 1912 Swimming and diving are added to the Olympics in Stockholm 1912 The Titanic sinks August 1914 World War I begins 1915 Einstein develops his general theory of relativity November 1917 Jeanette Rankin is the first woman elected to the U.S. Congress 1919 Treaty of Versailles ends World War I

TWO

The women's archery competition at the 1908 Olympic Games in London.

The Sporting Wo

For women, the twentieth century began with little evidence of progress. Their place was in the parlor, corseted and cosseted, restricted socially and politically. It was a time of extreme prudery, when legs were referred to as "limbs" and bare arms were considered prurient.

Faced with limited opportunities outside the sphere of home and family, Victorian female athletes were few in number. Any woman who did participate in sports was expected to be frail, modest, and reluctant to raise a drop of sweat on her brow. She was limited to the acceptable dress of the period, even while playing, and to noncompetitive activities. Archery, tennis, golf, figure skating, riding, and cycling were considered appropriately ladylike endeavors. Engaging in sports with men was often considered a function of courtship.

Women were allowed into the Olympic Games for the first time in Paris in 1900. Nineteen women competed in golf, tennis, or yachting, the only events open to women. Women's Olympic archery appeared in 1904 and then disappeared until 1972. Women's gymnastics were demonstrated for the third time but they were not considered an official event. Swimming and diving debuted in the 1912 Olympics in Stockholm, where fifty-seven women from eleven nations competed in swimming, diving, and tennis.

The women in the early Olympics had counterparts in society at large,

man

women who advanced the march toward equality. Isadora Duncan introduced a whole new idea of dance, while Mary Cassatt's paintings were well received in Paris. Marie Curie won a second Nobel Prize, and Helen Keller graduated from Radcliffe. However, strong prejudice against women continued in many aspects of society. A young Vassar College graduate was denied admission to Harvard University. Margaret Sanger, a public health nurse, was jailed for thirty days for opening a birth control clinic in Brooklyn, New York.

Women bobsledders in 1903.

With the outbreak of World War I, many women in the Western world entered the workforce for the first time. However, labor unions refused to admit them, and their health and pay were neglected. Employers considered it a woman's patriotic duty to leave her job as soon as the men returned from the war. It often seemed a case of one step forward and two steps back.

Australia's Annette Kellerman, born in 1886, took up swimming as therapy for her crippled legs. By 1900, she was winning awards at local swimming carnivals. Two years later, she won the New South Wales Ladies 100-yard and one-mile championships. There were few opportunities for women in competitive sport, so Kellerman turned to show business. She performed diving displays in Sydney and at the Melbourne Exhibition Aquarium, the "largest fish tank in the world."

When long-distance swimming began to fascinate the public, Kellerman toured Europe, swimming the Seine, the Danube, and other waterways. She tried to swim the English Channel and failed, but she became famous overnight. In 1910, she shocked the world when she swam Boston Harbor in an "indecent" one-piece bathing suit and was arrested for exposing her legs. She became a champion of women's rights, an advocate of physical fitness for women, and started a revolution in women's swimwear.

Annette Kellerman models the swimsuit she designed.

MARGARET ABBOTT

America's First Olympic Woman

The nineteen women who were first admitted to what would later be called the Olympic Games participated without the official consent of an Olympic Committee. Margaret Abbott was an American who happened to be in Paris studying art at the time. She read about the golf competition and decided to enter. She later told relatives that she won the tournament "because all the French girls apparently misunderstood the nature of the game scheduled for that day and turned up to play in high heels and tight skirts." Abbott happily accepted her prize for first, a bowl of old Saxon porcelain mounted in chiseled gold.

Golf in the United States in the 1890s was largely a pastime for the wealthy. The game was considered suitable for women because it was a noncontact activity and could be conducted in conventional dress. Society women, decked out in the most up-to-date outfits, wore long skirts, a shirt-waist starched, ironed and buttoned tightly around the neck and wrists, a tie or long scarf, a hat, and a girdle.

Abbott began playing golf in 1897 at a private club. Described as a "fierce competitor" with a "classy backswing," Abbott was coached by some of the best male amateurs of the day. Before winning the competition at the Paris Exposition, she established an impressive record in contests in her hometown of Chicago and throughout the Midwest.

Abbott married in 1902 and continued to play golf but not "seriously." She was hampered by a chronic knee ailment. When she died in 1955, Abbott was unaware of her place in history as the first American woman to compete in the Olympics.

American Margaret Abbott at the 1900 Olympic Games in Paris.

CHARLOTTE COOPER

First Woman to Win Gold

"Many a parent is prejudiced against her daughter having so much freedom, but my mother was lenient (and I consider most sensible) in that respect, and turned a deaf ear to anyone who advised her not to allow my sister and myself to travel about."—CHARLOTTE COOPER

Tennis had been "squeezed" into the Games largely because the women who played were well-bred and "ladylike." Women had been playing tennis with men for fifty years.

Charlotte "Chattie" Cooper was already a three-time Wimbledon champion when she represented Great Britain in the 1900 Olympic Games. Cooper was, according to a contemporary, Commander George Hillyard, "a quite unusually strong and active girl, with a constitution like the proverbial ostrich, who scarcely knew what it was to be tired, and was never sick or sorry." Her attacking game, unusual for the time, defeated the French champion, Helen Prevois, in straight sets. Cooper then went on to win a second "gold medal honor" in the mixed doubles with Reginald Doherty.

Cooper went on to take two more titles at Wimbledon, becoming the oldest player to win at Wimbledon when she was thirty-seven.

**Mrs. Sterry (Charlotte Cooper)
at Wimbledon.**

Madge Syers with Ulrich
Salchow, 1908.

MADGE SYERS

Women's Rights in Figure Skating

Britain's Madge Syers opened the door for women figure skaters by entering the all-male 1902 world championship and placing second behind Ulrich Salchow, the Swedish champion who pioneered the jump named after him. When Syers beat all but one male skater and proved that she was a good free skater, skating officials barred women from the championships. But in 1905, they decided to hold a separate "ladies" championship.

Syers learned to skate in Knightsbridge where, as a young girl, she joined the fashionable London Society. There she met her future husband, Edgar Syers, who trained her in the less rigid "international" style of skating. She was also a winning swimmer and equestrienne.

Syers won the first women's world skating championship in 1906 and again in 1907. She became the first female Olympic figure skating gold medalist at the London Games in 1908.

SARAH "FANNY" DURACK

Breaking Barriers

Prior to the 1912 Olympics, women athletes had never competed in what would be known as "swimming for ladies events." Swimming, like many sports, was thought unladylike and too physically demanding, and swimwear for women was considered too revealing.

Australia's Fanny Durack and her teammate, Mina Wylie, invaded this "bastion of male privilege" by becoming the first Australian women to compete at the Olympics and the first to swim for their country. Durack had set an unofficial world record for the 100-yard freestyle at the 1912 Australian Ladies' Championships. A month later, she beat her time by three seconds and received official recognition for a world record. Despite her stellar performance, many were fiercely opposed to sending her to the Olympics. Sending women to the Olympics, they said, was too expensive and a waste of money. The Olympics were "no place for a woman."

Durack and Wylie, on the other hand, felt they had as much right to go to the Olympic Games as any man. They had supporters, but many of them were primarily concerned with

From left, Fanny Durack, Mina Wylie, and Jennie Fletcher of Great Britain at the 1912 Olympic Games in Stockholm.

Australia becoming an athletic power and not with women's rights. Durack was a winner who could bring victory to her nation. In the end, after months of debate, the Australian Olympic Council voted to allow Durack to compete.

The struggle to get to the Olympics was far from over. Durack and Wylie had to find the money to finance the trip to Stockholm. Neither the Council nor the Australian government would assist the two women. The Durack and Wylie families carried much of the financial burden, raising enough money to send the swimmers and two chaperones.

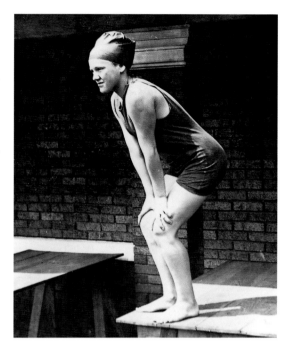

Fanny Durack at the 1912 Olympic Games in Stockholm.

Their efforts paid off. Durack set a world record in her heat and entered the semifinals a clear favorite. Although she swam a bit slower, she won her semifinal events easily, as did Wylie. When the swimmers hit the water in the finals of the 100-meter freestyle, Durack went out in front and never looked back. She won the gold medal and Wylie placed second, accounting for half the gold and silver medals won by Australia.

In Australia in the thirty years before the 1912 Olympics, a trend toward the liberation of women from the confines of "domesticity" and the pervasive image of the "dependent female" had been steadily gaining speed. Women's groups sprang up throughout Australia, fighting for temperance reform, the vote, and protective legislation for women and children.

As early as the 1880s, sport was "one of a number of bastions of male privilege to be invaded by women."* A wide range of women's sports clubs were established, including tennis, golf, cricket, and swimming. The first women's national golf championships were held in 1894. In 1895 *Cricket* magazine reported, "The new woman is taking up cricket evidently with the same energy which has characterized her other and more important spheres of life."

* Dennis H. Phillips, *Australian Women at the Olympic Games* (Kenthurst, New South Wales: Kangaroo Press, 1992).

THREE

The start of the infamous 800-meter race at the 1928 Olympic Games in Amsterdam.

A Place at the Ga

1920 TO 1947 The 1920s ushered in times of real change for women athletes and for women in general. Adventurous women broke the boundaries of pre-World War I standards. By the 1930s, independent women like painter Georgia O'Keeffe, anthropologist Margaret Mead, and actress Marlene Dietrich were bucking traditional female stereotypes and pursuing their careers outside the home. They enjoyed some professional and financial freedom and set an example for the future. People around the world hailed the success of Amelia Earhart when she became the first woman to fly across the Atlantic in 1928. Her fearlessness in what was considered a "masculine" endeavor captured the world's imagination in a way that Olympic women had yet to enjoy.

The 1920 Olympic Games saw more women competing in more events, but there remained restrictions and reprimands. U.S. figure skater Theresa Weld was scolded for including a salchow (jump) in her program. Women also competed in tennis, swimming, and diving, but track and field events were still considered masculine sports, "dangerous to the feminine nature" and better left to men with strength and speed.

In response, a group of French women staged their own international games, the "Jeux Olympiques Feminines du Monde," and in Monaco, a group

mes

of sportsmen sponsored the Olympiades Feminines. Three hundred women from five countries competed in track and field events and played basketball in the Jeux Feminins, which were so successful they were held again in 1922 and 1923.

It was another five years before track and field events for women were added to the Olympic Games. The five new events in 1928 included an 800-meter race. When several women reportedly collapsed at the end of that race, public reaction was so strong that the 800-meter race for women was discontinued until 1960.

The 1924 Olympics were the first in which sports were organized by their international governing bodies. Fencing was introduced for women, along with two more swimming events. However, it was the last year for tennis until 1988, a decision made by the tennis federations in response to the appalling conditions at the Games. This was also the first year for the Winter Games, a designation made retroactively on an event called International Sports Week. The only women's competition was figure skating.

The first American Olympic Games were held in Los Angeles in 1932. Despite the Depression, new facilities, including the first Olympic Village, were created. The village was for men only. There were no new sports for women, but two track and field events were added. Louise Stokes and Tidye Pickett became the first two African-American women to qualify for the Games but they were not allowed to participate.

The 1936 Games in Berlin, presided over by Hitler, were the most politicized Games to date. Gymnastics was the new sport for women.

With the outbreak of World War II, the Olympic Games were cancelled for 1940 and 1946. Women were called upon to support the war effort by working in factories, flying transport planes, rationing the disappearing supplies of coffee, butter, sugar, coal and gasoline, holding scrap metal drives, selling war bonds, tending victory gardens, and assuming the jobs of men, some of whom would never return. In the United States, more than two million women entered the workforce.

"Rosie the Riveter" became an American symbol for women getting equal pay for equal work in the war effort. But where would they go from there?

Fashion designer Gabrielle "Coco" Chanel freed women from the confines of their clothing and uncluttered their wardrobes. Beginning in the 1920s, she used comfortable fabrics in subdued colors for her clothing designs. Frustrated with trying to keep her long hair clean, she cut it in a bob, and millions of women followed suit. In the 1930s, she set another major trend when she came back from a vacation with a deep tan and wearing slacks. She called her famous perfume No. 5 because a fortune teller told her it was her lucky number.

Chanel was one of the most imitated fashion designers. She set many revolutionary trends for women in fashion and enjoyed a major resurgence of popularity in 1954.

August–September 1920   Suzanne Lenglen revolutionizes women's tennis   August 1920   19th amendment passes and American women win the right to vote   May 1921   Jeux Feminins, the first all-women Olympics, opens in Monaco   October 1921   Alice Milliat and members of Femina Sport form the Federation Sportive Feminine Internationale   August 1922   The Federation Sportive sponsors an international track and field competition for women in Paris   March 1923   Actress Sarah Bernhardt dies   February 1923   Blues singer Bessie Smith makes her first recording   January 1924   First Winter Olympics in Chamonix and the debut of eleven-year-old figure skater Sonja Henie   August 1924   First Summer Olympics are held in Paris and fencing for women is introduced   November 1924   Texan Miriam "Ma" Ferguson is elected first woman governor in the U.S.   August 1926   Gertrude Ederle, first woman to swim the English Channel, sets the record in 14 hours, 31 minutes   1927 Clara Bow becomes the "It" girl   May 1927   Charles Lindberg completes first nonstop solo flight across the Atlantic   September 1927   Babe Ruth hits his sixtieth home run   October 1927   Al Jolson stars in *The Jazz Singer*   January 1928   Sonja Henie introduces ballet into figure skating and wins her first gold medal   June 1928   Amelia Earhart is the first woman to fly across the Atlantic   August 1928   Track and field for women makes its debut at the Amsterdam Summer Games   October 1929   The stock market crashes and the Great Depression begins   1930   Gandhi leads the Salt March in defiance of British rule in India   January 1932   Speed skating for women is demonstrated at the Lake Placid Winter Games   August 1932   At the Los Angeles Games, Babe Didrikson is the first woman to win medals in three events, and Louise Stokes and Tidye Pickett are the first African-American women to qualify, but they do not compete   1933   Adolph Hitler is named German chancellor   January 1936 Women's alpine skiing is introduced at the Winter Games   August 1936   At the Berlin Olympics, Helene Mayer is the only Jew to compete for Germany   1939–1945   World War II   1945   Eleanor Roosevelt becomes a delegate to the United Nations

AMERICAN SWIMMERS AND DIVERS

A Swimming Monopoly

The widespread popularity of swimming and diving in the United States at the beginning of the twentieth century led to the birth of swimming clubs throughout the country. Young boys and girls flocked to these clubs and, from the pool of talented swimmers, America built a dynasty of talented competitors who took the Olympics by storm in 1920 and never looked back.

American women divers won three out of six medals at the Antwerp Games in 1920. They gained momentum at Paris four years later when they seized five out of six medals, and they repeated their record in Amsterdam in 1928. Similarly, the United States' women swimmers made a huge splash when they won seven out of nine swimming medals at the 1920 Games.

Ethelda Bleibtrey was America's first female Olympic swimming champion and the only person ever to win all the women's swimming events at any Olympic Games. Bleibtrey won three gold medals at Antwerp in 1920. She had several other firsts, including an arrest for swimming "in the nude" at Manhattan Beach. Bleibtrey had removed her long woolen stockings

American swimmers bound for the 1924 Olympic Games in Paris.

24

before entering the water. Positive public opinion was so strong that she was released from jail, and women everywhere were freed from swimming in stockings.

Another American swimmer who charted new territory was Gertrude Ederle. In 1922, Ederle broke seven world records at various distances. And in 1926, she became the first woman to swim the English Channel. According to Ripley's "Believe It or Not," she was met on the beach at Dover by an English immigration officer who demanded her passport. Ederle was so popular with the American public that she became a household name. At the 1924 Games in Paris, Ederle took the bronze in both the 100-meter and 400-meter freestyle.

Helen Wainwright was originally chosen to try the English Channel swim and had to back out because of a pulled muscle. Prior to the Channel swim, she had become the only athlete to win Olympic medals in both diving and swimming. She took the silver in the three-meter springboard at the 1920 Games and a silver in the 400-meter freestyle at the 1924 Games.

Diver Helen Meany dominated American diving longer than any other woman. She competed in three Olympics, winning the gold medal in springboard diving in 1928.

Before Martha Norelius turned professional, she became the first woman swimmer to win gold medals in two different Olympics—she received her first in 1924 when she was fifteen, and her second in 1928. During the summer of 1927, she set twenty-nine world swimming records. Norelius was considered the first woman to have a swimming style like a man's. The high position of her head, her arched back, and her heavy six-beat kick helped her hydroplane over the water. For eight years, Norelius held the record for being the world's fastest woman swimmer at any distance.

The United States diving team captured all the springboard diving medals from 1920, the first year the event was included, through the 1948 Olympics in London. They also dominated platform diving, winning the majority of medals through 1956. Many of them—Elizabeth Becker, Georgia Coleman, Dorothy Poynton-Hill, and more—took medals in both events.

From left, American divers Marjorie Gestring, Georgia Coleman, and Dorothy Poynton-Hill.

SUZANNE LENGLEN

A New Way to Play Tennis

France's Suzanne Lenglen set the pace in women's tennis and shattered its Victorian decorum with her so-called unfeminine athleticism and unconventional garb—short skirts, cosmetics, and jeweled headbands. For the 1920 Olympic Games, Lenglen jettisoned the customary corset, hat, and long cotton shirt for a short pleated skirt, silk stockings rolled above the knee, a sleeveless silk blouse, matching sweater, and a bandeau. Her passion for glamour and style captivated the crowds. Her fluid, flawless play won her two gold medals and a bronze.

As the reigning Wimbledon and Olympic champion, Lenglen became the first female athlete to attain celebrity status. Every move she made was reported in the press. Although an amateur, she was allowed to endorse products such as the Lenglen tennis shoe and to write for newspapers and magazines.

The French loved her style, her savoir-faire, and most of all, they loved how she moved on the tennis court. Lenglen was graceful and poised, with the mind of a chess master who "saw" her moves before she made them. "Lenglen danced tennis. She celebrated tennis. She laughed and she sang tennis . . . because she was so unlike any other tennis player in the world, no one ever said that this goddess 'played tennis.'"*

By the end of 1925, Lenglen had established a record of dominance in tennis unequaled in that or any other sport. She had won fifteen World Hard Court Championships, fifteen French National Championships, six Wimbledon titles, and three Olympic medals. Lenglen was a true national heroine who enjoyed the prestige and influence of royalty in France and whose talent and personality were recognized around the world. Today, Lenglen is still considered one of the greatest tennis players that ever lived.

*Larry Engleman, *The Goddess and the American Girl* (New York: Oxford University Press, 1988).

**Tennis world champion
Suzanne Lenglen in 1923.**

KINUE HITOMI

First Asian Champion

Japan's Kinue Hitomi burst onto the international sports scene at a time when women's athletics was still a very controversial subject, thought to lead to premature aging, even sterility. Despite the controversy, Hitomi, born in 1907, grew up a "tomboy" whose favorite sport was tennis. Athletically gifted, she was sent to the only physical education school for women in Japan. There she became a great all-around athlete, excelling in sprinting, jumping, and the discus.

In 1924 at the age of seventeen, Hitomi set her first of many world records in the triple jump. Eventually, she would best all other female athletes in twelve different events. Winning two gold medals in the second World Women's Games in 1926 brought her international recognition. Hitomi participated in the 1928 Olympics and won the silver in the infamous 800-meter race after which several women fainted, causing the Olympic Committee to ban races over 200 meters for women until 1960.

Hitomi was the Japanese team captain in the 1930 Prague Women's Games, winning all of Japan's fifteen points. She won two gold medals, one silver, and one bronze, and was awarded a gold medal as the best all-around athlete.

In 1931, she was diagnosed with tuberculosis and died later that year at the age of twenty-four. Her accomplishments have stood the test of time: history hails Hitomi as the first great female all-around athlete.

Kinue Hitomi in the 800-meter race at the 1928 Olympic Games in Amsterdam.

HELENE MAYER

Olympian Athlete Caught in Politics

When Helene Mayer was born in Offenbach, Germany, in 1911, to a Christian mother and Jewish father, her parents never imagined the place their daughter would occupy in history. Helene began taking fencing lessons as a child and won the German foil championship when she was just thirteen years old. Four years later, she won eighteen bouts and lost two to win the gold medal at the 1928 Olympic Games. She went on to become the world foil champion in 1929 and 1931.

Representing Germany in the 1932 Games in Los Angeles, California, the statuesque young woman with green eyes and blond hair placed a disappointing fifth. With her fencing career on hold, Helene decided to remain in Los Angeles to study international law at the University of Southern California. Then, in late 1933, she learned she had been expelled from the Offenbach Fencing Club. The announcement coincided with the onset of Hitler's racial politics. In response, the International Olympic Committee threatened to cancel the 1936 Games, scheduled for Berlin, unless the discrimination against Jewish athletes ended.

Helene Mayer at the 1932 Olympic Games in Los Angeles.

Many protested Hitler's discrimination and there were threats to boycott the Games. Under pressure, Germany invited exiled ice hockey player Rudi Hall and fencer Helene Mayer to compete as members of Germany's Olympic team.

Mayer issued a statement saying she would be pleased to represent Germany because she had done so before and because she was eager to visit her family. The German government declared Mayer an "Aryan."

Thirty-one nations sent a total of 300 fencers to the 1936 Games in Berlin. The eliminations went on for two weeks. Stamina replaced patience and ability as the quality that mattered most. By the end of the grueling competition, only eight women were left, Mayer among them. In the final competition, Mayer was defeated by Ilona Elek, a Hungarian Jew, and took a silver medal.

The world waited to see if gold medalist Elek would salute the führer upon receiving her medal. She did not, but Helene Mayer, ascending the winners' platform, held her blond head high and her body rigid in the traditional "Heil Hitler!" salute.

SONJA HENIE

"Pavlova of the Ice"

Sonja Henie, the only woman in history to win three gold medals in Olympic figure skating, took to the ice at age six and loved it. The diminutive Norwegian began competing a year later against skaters twice her age. By the age of nine, she had become the champion of Norway. "I've never seen a little girl so determined to skate, and with the ability to do it with so much sparkle and verve," said an early coach, Oscar Holte.

Henie competed in her first Olympics in 1924 at age eleven. She placed last, but as the youngest competitor, she charmed the world with her grace and style. Henie's idol was the ballerina Anna Pavlova, and she made it her goal to become a dancer on ice. Within a year, she was the youngest girl ever to win a world championship. Thousands of Norwegians, including King Haakon and Queen Maude, cheered her on. In 1928, Henie won her first gold medal in skating at the St. Moritz Olympics.

Henie's parents were supportive of their daughter and they handled her career shrewdly. In 1930, they took Sonja to New York to compete in the world championships at Madison Square Garden. Henie won the competition and the hearts of Americans, who called her "New York's Scandinavian Sweetheart." Henie went on to win gold medals at the 1932 and 1936 Olympics and eight more world championships.

After the 1936 Games, she turned professional and launched her first ice show in Hollywood, where she was a sensation. Darryl F. Zanuck of 20th Century Fox signed Henie and her skates to a movie contract. Her first film, *One in a Million*, was a box office smash. Henie became a U.S. citizen and went on to make ten more movies and to tour with her own Hollywood Ice Revue. Her energy and seemingly effortless artistry encouraged the public to flock to local ice rinks in record numbers. The "Pavlova of the Ice" had accomplished what she'd set out to do: thanks to Henie, ice skating became one of the most popular sports around the world.

Stanislawa Walasiewicz was born in Poland, but grew up in Cleveland, Ohio, as Stella Walsh. She remained a Polish citizen just long enough to compete for Poland in the 1932 Olympic Games. She won a gold medal in the 100-meter race.

In Berlin four years later, a favorite to win, she was defeated by the six-foot American runner, Helen Stephens, and ended with a silver medal. A Polish journalist accused Stephens of being a man, and in response the German officials issued a statement that she had passed a sex text. Many years later, Walsh was shot to death during a robbery, and the autopsy revealed that it was Walsh who was actually a man.

Sonja Henie.

30

ETHEL CATHERWOOD

"The Saskatoon Lily"

The Amsterdam Games of 1928 marked the first official Olympic track and field competitions for women. Included in the program were the discus, the high jump, the 100-meter and 200-meter sprints, the 4 x 100-meter relay, and the 800-meter run. Women's appearance on the Amsterdam track was met with more than a little resistance, and one of the issues was modesty. It was stipulated that the women wear shorts that came within 12 centimeters (about 4 inches) of the knee.

The most famous of the first women track and field Olympians was eighteen-year-old Ethel Catherwood, known as the "The Saskatoon Lily" from Canada. After taking the gold medal with a jump of 5 feet, 2½ inches, she returned home a heroine. The provincial government awarded her a trust fund of $3,000; however, the money was not to be used for training in track and field but to help her with her piano studies.

When asked if she would pursue a motion picture contract, Catherwood—a beautiful young woman—replied, "I'd rather gulp poison . . ."

Ethel Catherwood at the 1928 Olympic Games in Amsterdam.

ELIZABETH ROBINSON

First Female Track Gold Medalist

Betty Robinson's life is a great comeback story. She was discovered running for the train that took her to school. "The coach of the track team watched out of the window of the train as I caught up to it and suggested that I should develop my talent," Robinson said. "Till then I didn't even know there were women's races."

At the 1928 Amsterdam Games, Robinson was the only American to make it to the finals in one of the newly introduced track and field events, the 100-meter race. A sixteen-year-old student from Riverdale, Illinois, Robinson was not favored. After two false starts, two women—Canadian and German—were disqualified. Robinson was left to face Fanny Rosenfeld, the favorite, and two other runners. In a close finish, Robinson was declared the winner and became the first woman to win a gold medal in track and field in the Olympics. A few days later, Robinson anchored the U.S. 4 x 100-meter relay team for a second place finish behind the Canadians.

Robinson's career was off and running, and she looked forward to competing again in the 1932 Games, but it was not to be. In 1931, Robinson was in a serious airplane accident that left her in a coma for almost two months. She suffered injuries to her arm, leg, and head. Once

Betty Robinson wins the 100-meter race at the 1928 Olympic Games in Amsterdam.

awake and on the mend, Robinson hoped to compete again. Although she could not bend her knee down "on the mark," she worked hard at her rehabilitation. Two years after the accident, she started running again and was named to the U.S. 4 x 100-meter relay team for the 1936 Berlin Olympics.

Once more, Robinson and her teammates were not the favorites. The German team set a world record in a preliminary heat and was winning by ten meters over the U.S. runners. In the final race, as Robinson tells it, "the Germans were about ten meters ahead when I was about to pass the baton to Helen (Stephens). But then I saw the German girl throw her arms to her head and break down crying. She had dropped the baton." Robinson and her teammates won the gold.

BABE DIDRIKSON

Texas Tornado

"She was the sort of woman who took off tight shoes which hurt and wiggled her toes, no matter where she was . . . . the first athlete to make people confront issues of femininity: how much muscle is too much? how much is unfeminine?" —ADRIANNE BLUE, *Faster, Higher, Further*

Mildred "Babe" Didrikson, a high school dropout from Beaumont, Texas, is considered America's greatest woman athlete from the first half of the twentieth century. The sixth of seven children, she was gifted at every sport she tried. She hit so many home runs as a young girl that someone compared her to Babe Ruth and the nickname "Babe" stuck.

When Didrikson was sixteen, an insurance company basketball scout saw her play and made her a dual offer of a job as a stenographer and a position on an "amateur" company basketball team. After some discussion, her father gave her permission to go ahead. She turned out to be a wise investment, bringing the Dallas Cyclones a second-place finish in the national basketball championships and loads of free advertising for the insurance company.

By the time the 1932 national track and field athletics championships (which were also the Olympic trials) rolled around, Didrikson's reputation was well known. She was allowed to compete in as many events as she liked. "It was one of those days when you know you could fly," Babe recalled. Within three hours, she won five events, tied a sixth, and chalked up two world records. The press called it "the most amazing series of performances ever accomplished by an individual, male or female, in track and field history."

Babe Didrikson high jumps at the 1932 Olympic Games in Los Angeles.

Didrikson was one of 127 women who participated in the 1932 Games in Los Angeles. "I came out here to beat everybody in sight, and that is exactly what I'm going to do," she said. But Olympic rules limited her to three events. In the first event, fifty thousand people watched as she broke the javelin record by more than four feet for the gold medal. Two days later, in a photo-finish, Babe won her second gold, with an 11.7-second world mark in the 80-meter hurdles. As she prepared for the high jump, she told the press, "I don't know who my opponents are and, anyways, it wouldn't make any difference. I hope they are good."

The field of high jumpers was good. As the bar was raised to 5 feet 5¼ inches, Didrikson and teammate Jean Shiley were the only two left in the competition. Both women made clean jumps, setting a new world record. The bar was raised an inch. Babe cleared it but kicked one of the uprights on the landing. The bar fell, and the judges ruled no jump. Shiley failed to clear the bar. It was lowered an inch, and both jumpers cleared it again. The judges, who had to decide whether the two women should share the gold, declared that they would share the world record, but that Didrikson's last jump was illegal because she had dived (a method of jumping she'd used throughout the competition). Shiley was awarded the gold medal, and Babe took the silver.

Following the Olympics, Babe went professional and made good earnings. The press began to question why she didn't have a man to support her. Then in 1938, she married a wrestler, George Zaharias. Married life didn't stop her from becoming the finest and most famous woman golfer of her generation. She beat every other woman on the golf tour.

By the end of her career, she had excelled at a dozen different sports, held American, Olympic, or world records in five different track and field events between 1930 and 1932, and won a total of eighty-two golf tournaments. She ranked high enough as a basketball player to be given the honorary title of All-American. She could swim close to world-record time on short distances, and she carried a .400 batting average in a Dallas softball league. She was phenomenal.

Early in the century, when women who participated in the Olympic Games were few in number, their presence was new and at least some of their stories were recorded. By the end of the 1930s, women in the Olympics numbered in the hundreds, and ironically very little is known about some of the top athletes.

In 1920, Magda Julin-Mauroy of Sweden won the figure skating singles gold. In 1924, Ellen Osiier of Denmark took the gold in fencing, winning all sixteen of her matches. Lina Radke, from Germany, won the infamous 800-meter race in 1928, and Helen Konopacka of Poland was the first woman gold medalist in the discus throw. Hideko Maehata was the first Japanese woman to win a medal in Olympic swimming and one of the first to win using the controversial butterfly stroke. Hendrika Mastenbroek of the Netherlands won medals in four swimming events—three gold and one silver—in 1936.

Many remarkable women have participated in the Olympics throughout the century, some quietly and some with a splash.

(Above) Hideko Maehata (foreground) at the 1936 Olympic Games in Berlin.

(Left) Hendrika Maestenbroek at the 1936 Olympic Games in Berlin.

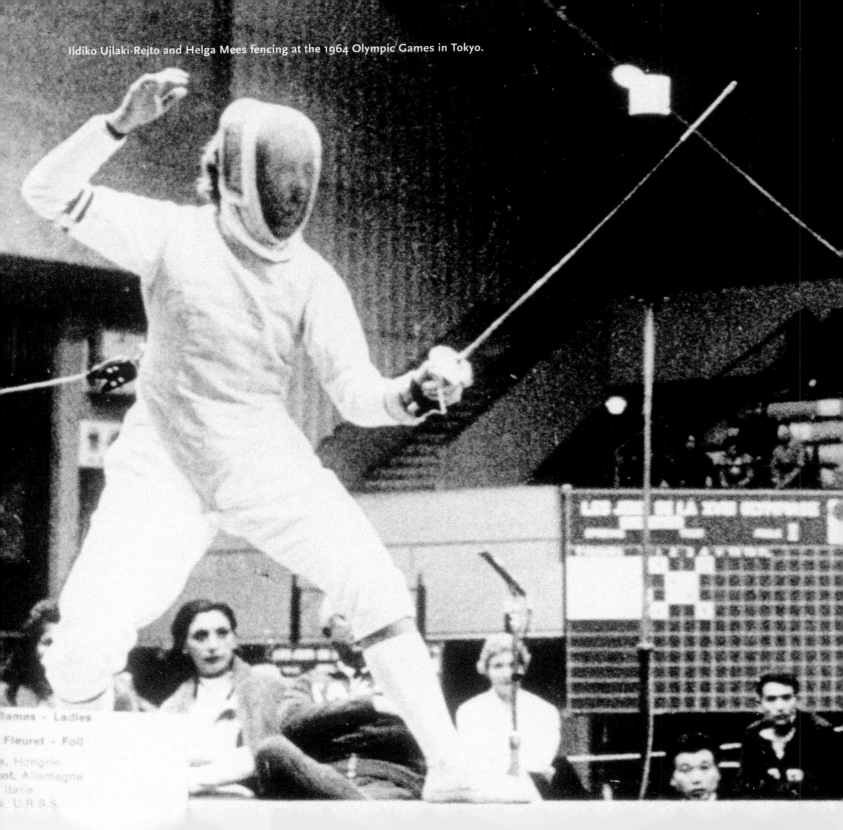

Ildiko Ujlaki-Rejto and Helga Mees fencing at the 1964 Olympic Games in Tokyo.

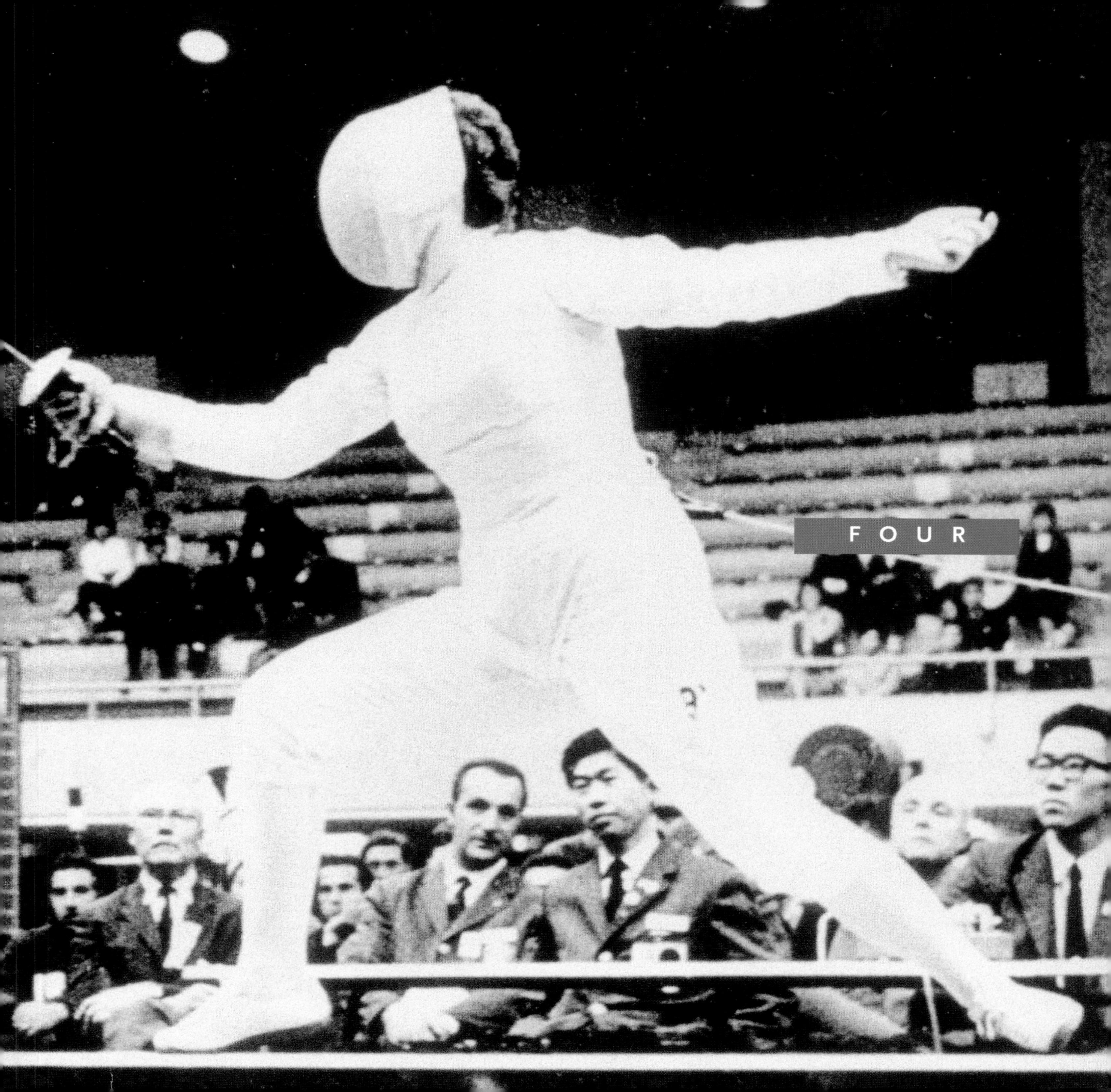

FOUR

Conflicting Ima

1948 TO 1971 The first Olympics after World War II were held in London in 1948. The world had changed significantly during the twelve-year hiatus. Women who had swarmed into the workplace to perform many of the functions of absent men returned home in large numbers, finding themselves back in an apron and behind a baby carriage. Many women regarded this abrupt change as a step backward, and their frustrations with limited opportunities ignited the modern feminist movement.

As feminism grew, the roles of women began to change. In the sports arena, women found that it was slowly becoming more acceptable to be an athlete. Colleges began to promote competitive sports for women, albeit using "girls" rules in team sports, tennis, and track and field. Professional women athletes received less pay than their male counterparts, and track and field sports were still frowned upon because of their strenuous, competitive nature.

Conflicting roles and images encompassed African-Americans as well. There was rioting over jobs, housing, and treatment of blacks in the armed services, while the civil rights movement brought many African-Americans together in their struggle for equality. In 1950, tennis player Althea Gibson

ges

became the first African-American to compete in the U.S. tennis championships. Against the backdrop of the civil rights turmoil of the 1960s, Wilma Rudolph and other African-American Olympians turned in the most stunning successes of the Games.

During the more than two decades between the 1948 Olympic Games and 1972, many new sports for women were added to Olympic competition, such as gymnastics and volleyball. The number of women athletes continued to increase. There was also growing recognition of women's importance and abilities off the athletic field. Feminism spread from America, Europe, and Australia to all corners of the world. Ceylon had the world's first elected woman leader in 1960. In 1966, Indira Gandhi became the second woman to head a nation in the modern world.

Still, the expectations of women were divided and confusing—role models as diverse as Marilyn Monroe, Indira Gandhi, "Barbie," and Betty Friedan shared the public eye. Women struggled to define their roles, while in society at large the messages were mixed. Strong or weak? Sexy or athletic? Active or passive? Grace and glory seemed to remain on opposite sides of the coin.

January 1948 Mahatma Gandhi is assassinated Gretchen Fraser wins the first American gold medal in skiing at St. Moritz August 1948 Alice Coachman wins the high jump—the first woman of color to win an Olympic gold medal September 1949 Soviet Union creates their first atomic bomb October 1949 China establishes the People's Republic 1950 Korean War begins August 1950 Florence Chadwick breaks Ederle's Channel record Althea Gibson is the first African-American woman admitted to the U.S. Tennis Association March 1951 The Rosenbergs are found guilty July 1952 Argentina mourns the early death of Eva Peron August 1952 Soviet women dominate the newly introduced gymnastics at the Helsinki Games Women compete in equestrian events for the first time May 1953 Jacqueline Cochran is the first woman to break the sound barrier June 1953 Elizabeth II is crowned monarch of England 1954 Gwendolyn Brooks is the first African-American to win the Pulitzer Prize December 1955 Rosa Parks is arrested January 1956 Tenley Albright, recovering from polio, wins the gold medal in figure skating at the Games in Cortina d'Ampezzo, Italy August 1956 At the Melbourne Games, Juliana Clemenal-Minuzzo is the first woman to recite the Olympic oath Larissa Latynina of the Soviet Union wins the first of eighteen medals in gymnastics October 1957 Sputnik is launched by the Soviet Union January 1960 Speed skating is introduced for women in Squaw Valley, California Carol Heiss performs the first double jump in women's figure skating August 1960 Wilma Rudolph wins three gold medals in Rome Sirimavo Bandaranaike becomes prime minister of Ceylon, the first woman elected to lead a nation August 1961 Berlin Wall is built 1963 Betty Friedan writes *The Feminine Mystique* January 1964 At the Games in Innsbruck, Austria, Ortrun Enderlein of Germany wins the first gold medal in women's luge August 1964 Olympic volleyball is introduced in Tokyo, where the Japanese women's team begins a winning legacy January 1966 Indira Gandhi is elected first woman prime minister of India January 1968 The Olympic Committee conducts gender tests for the first time in Grenoble, France August 1968 Enriquetta Basilio is the first woman to light the Olympic flame in Mexico City American women take medals in every swimming event November 1968 Shirley Chisholm is the first African-American woman elected to the U.S. House of Representatives 1969 Gold Meir is elected Israel's first woman prime minister July 1969 Men walk on the moon

BARBARA ANN SCOTT

Champion of a Golden Age

Barbara Ann Scott's fairy princess looks made her the idol of little girls everywhere. The nineteen-year-old European figure skating champion from Ottawa, Canada, inspired the Barbara Ann Scott doll, a 1940s version of the Barbie doll.

Barbara Ann Scott.

Although a Canadian, Scott was persuaded by the Europeans to compete for them in the 1947 and 1948 European Championships. (The practice of allowing non-Europeans to compete ended after Scott and Dick Button won the European titles.) Scott's dainty, precise but athletic style helped create what was called the "golden age" of skating, the years from 1947 to 1961 when the Canadians and the Americans dominated the sport.

Scott won the Olympic gold medal at the 1948 St. Moritz Winter Games. Her championship was the culmination of extensive training. She had worked long and hard to be the best in the world and her efforts paid off.

MICHELINE OSTERMEYER

Olympian Athlete and Concert Musician

The multitalented Micheline Ostermeyer thrilled fans both on the athletic field and in the concert hall. Born in 1922 in Rang-du-Fliers, France, Ostermeyer moved to Tunisia with her family in 1929. A promising pianist, she moved back to France at age fourteen to study music at the Paris Conservatory. When World War II started, she returned to Tunisia, where she joined the French Athletic Association and competed in several track and field events locally and internationally. But music was her first love, and at the end of the war, Ostermeyer went back

Micheline Ostermeyer high jumps at the 1948 Olympic Games in London.

Micheline Ostermeyer at the piano.

to France to complete her music studies and begin concert tours.

As the 1948 Olympics approached, the French team needed someone to throw the discus. They asked Ostermeyer if she would compete for France. She had thrown the discus only one time competitively and was afraid she would appear ridiculous. With the help of four coaches hired to train her for the Olympics, Ostermeyer agreed to give the event a shot. She came up a winner, capturing a gold medal in the shot put and a bronze in the high jump.

Ostermeyer continued to compete until she suffered a severe muscle strain in 1951. She married the next year and moved to Lebanon with her husband, where she taught piano and resumed her career as a concert pianist. A little more than a decade later, her husband died, and she returned to France to teach music at a conservatory just outside of Paris.

FRANCINA "FANNY" BLANKERS-KOEN

The "Marvelous Mama"

It had been twelve years since the 1936 Olympics when the Games resumed in 1948. When World War II ended and the men returned home, most women were forced to leave their jobs outside the home and go back to aprons and baby carriages. When a woman like Blankers-Koen insisted on juggling both mothering and athletic training, the press had a field day.

Dutch runner Fanny Blankers-Koen, who competed in the 1936 Olympics at age eighteen, had grown up, married, and had two children. At age thirty, the sports world said she was too old to compete. She was accused of neglecting her son and daughter, even though she had the full support of her husband and coach, Jan. "My wife is a real housewife," Jan said. "She cooks, cleans and takes care of our children. She sews and knits their clothes." Unyielding in the face of criticism, Blankers-Koen refused to cave in under the pressure.

Her determination paid off. Blankers-Koen sprinted her way to gold medals in the 80-meter hurdles, the 100-meter dash, and the 200-meter dash. She won yet another gold medal anchoring the Dutch relay team in the 4 x 100-meter relay. And these events were not even her best. Olympic rules limited women to three individual events. Blankers-Koen never had a chance to show the world what she could do in the high jump and long jump.

Fanny Blankers-Koen (right) at the 1948 Olympic Games in London.

The response? The headline in the *London Daily Graphic* read, "Fastest Woman in the World Is an Expert Cook." While Blankers-Koen's abilities as an athlete captured the world's imagination, it was her dual role that got the attention.

ALICE COACHMAN

First Black Woman Worldwide to Win an Olympic Gold

In 1946, African-American track athlete Alice Coachman became the first woman of color chosen to be a member of the U.S. All-American Track and Field team. She underwent "careful scrutiny" before being selected and was found to be "quiet, ladylike, reserved and most desirable," qualities befitting the then current image of women in sports.

There were only twelve women on the track and field team at the U.S. Olympic Trials in 1948, and nine of them were African-Americans, an unprecedented representation at the time.

As they sailed toward London on the *SS America*, the team's spirits were high. But after the Games began, their spirits were quickly dampened. "I was disgusted," said Coachman, "because we thought we had some of the fastest girls, and they kept getting eliminated." By the last day of the Olympics, only one U.S. woman had earned a medal—a bronze. Coachman's turn came two days later.

The competition dragged on in the high jump until only Coachman and two other women—one French, one British—were left. The crowd, more than 50,000 people, most of them English, had high hopes of seeing Dorothy Tyler (Odam) of Great Britain take the gold. At this point, neither Great Britain nor the United States had captured a gold in track and field. Ostermeyer of France was first to be elimi-

The U.S. track and field team at the 1948 Olympic Games in London.

nated, and the excitement increased. Both Tyler and Coachman missed the bar at 5 feet 6½ inches, and Coachman had had fewer misses at 5 feet 6¼ inches—an Olympic record. Thus she won the gold medal, the only one for the U.S. team, and became the first African-American woman in U.S. Olympic history to take home a gold.

Once back home, Coachman was greeted as a true champion. Parades were thrown in her honor, and she was awarded a full scholarship to complete college education. Coachman took her fame in stride. She had accomplished her goals as an athlete and went on to pursue her goal of becoming a teacher.

SHIRLEY STRICKLAND

"Aussie Gold"

"As an athlete, I believe I was popular as long as I was demure, appreciative, decorative, obedient, and winning." —SHIRLEY STRICKLAND DE LA HUNTY (1989)

Shirley Strickland, born in 1925 in the wheat belt of Western Australia, competed in the 1948 Games, the first Olympic competition following World War II. One of only five women chosen to represent Australia, Strickland was well aware of the postwar campaign compelling women to devote themselves entirely to home and family. Women could excel in "outside" activities, like sports, but they were never to compromise their femininity. "I well remember wearing exotic hairstyles and Chanel No. 5 during my competitive days to reassure myself, as well as everyone else, that I was female."

At age twelve, Strickland went away to boarding school. There she participated in a wide variety of sports but was even more interested in academics. At the University of Western Australia, she was refused admission to the school of engineering because there were no female toilets in the building, so she turned her attention to nuclear physics and earned a degree with

Shirley Strickland at the 1956 Olympic Games in Melbourne.

honors. While at the university, she felt "the need for both mental and physical challenges" and began participating in track and field events. In the 1947 State Championships, she proved herself to be Australia's most promising athlete, male or female.

Strickland was teaching physics and math at Perth Technical College when she was asked to represent Australia in the Olympics in 1948. When she stepped onto the Olympic track at London's Wembley Stadium, it was her first international meet. The field of runners included the Netherlands' Fanny Blankers-Koen, a veteran of the 1936 Olympics. "There was an enormous sense of pressure and emotion," Strickland said. "It was a remarkably exciting experience."

Blankers-Koen took the gold in four events, with Strickland winning a silver and two bronze medals. Strickland was not deterred. She returned to Olympic competition in 1952 and won the 80-meter hurdles and took a bronze in the 100 meters.

Then, in 1956 at the Melbourne Olympic Games, Strickland won two gold medals and became the first woman in history to win track and field gold medals in successive Olympics. "Most of my big races have been in other countries," she said, after gliding to a decisive victory in the 80-meter hurdles. "You have no idea how thrilling it is to win at home."

LIS HARTEL

Riding Jubilee

Women were allowed to compete in equestrian sports for the first time in Olympic history at the 1952 Helsinki Games. At that time, equestrian events became some of the few that are "open" sports—where men and women compete against each other.

Among the riders was Lis Hartel, a remarkable Danish woman who had been stricken with polio eight years earlier. The sudden paralysis could have marked the end of her promising career as one of Denmark's leading equestrians, but Hartel was determined to walk and ride again. After only eight months of intensive and painful rehabilitation, she was able to hobble along with the help of crutches. Her first time back on a horse left her so exhausted that she needed two weeks to recuperate before trying again.

Hartel remained paralyzed below the knees and needed assistance to get on and off her horse, Jubilee. Still, only three years after her bout with polio, she finished second in the indi-

Lis Hartel at the 1952 Olympic Games in Helsinki.

vidual dressage event at the Scandinavian riding championships. Then in 1952 in Helsinki, Hartel took her place as the first woman Olympic medalist in dressage, winning a silver medal to Henri Saint Cyr's gold. In an inspiring and poignant moment, Cyr helped Hartel off her horse and up onto the podium for the medal presentation.

Four years later, Hartel won a second silver medal in individual dressage at the Stockholm Games.

PAT McCORMICK

One Tough Lady

Pat McCormick remembers spending her childhood playing and swimming in the Pacific Ocean. She and her older brother liked to hang out at California's famous Muscle Beach, where they worked out with the weight lifters who congregated there and eventually performed in weekend shows. "Muscle Beach really helped me later as a diver because I became physically

strong," Pat said. "My mother tried to get me to be more ladylike, but I was a tomboy."

McCormick started competing in swimming and diving competitions at age eleven; at sixteen, she was the champion of Long Beach, California. Although strong and athletic, McCormick did not have any formal training. That changed in 1947 when Aileen Allen, a coach at the Los Angeles Athletic Club, saw her diving and invited her to join the club. "She couldn't point her toes and she couldn't straighten out her body," said Sammy Lee, a two-time Olympic champion who trained at the club. "All she had was physical strength." That same year, Pat met Glenn McCormick, a wrestler and gymnast at the University of Southern California. He used his gymnastics training to coach Pat on the diving board. A year later, they were married. The partnership paid off. In 1947, Pat was a surprise runner-up in platform diving at the national championships. In 1948, she was a close fourth in the Olympic trials. "That defeat was the greatest thing that ever happened to me because all of a sudden I knew I could win the Olympics," McCormick said. McCormick went to work.

She was one tough lady. Her exhausting training routine included 80 to 100 dives per day, six days a week. Nothing, not even injuries, could slow her down. During a medical examination, a doctor discovered a six-inch scar on her scalp, several scars at the base of her spine, blood welts across her collarbone from the impact of the water, lacerations of the feet and elbows, a loose jaw, and chips on all her front teeth. "I've seen worse casualty cases, but only where a building caved in," the doctor told her.

In 1951, at the age of twenty-two, McCormick became the first diver ever to win all five national championships. She competed that year in her first Olympic Games in Helsinki. She won a gold medal in springboard diving and a second gold in platform diving.

Pat McCormick.

Following the Olympics, she refused offers to turn professional and set her sights on winning another pair of gold medals four years later. However, she didn't wait to have a child. Only five months before the 1956 Olympic trials, McCormick gave birth to her first baby. Her pregnancy didn't slow her down. She continued to train and swim up to two days before the birth. Once again, her perseverance paid off. She won the platform and springboard diving events at the Olympic trials.

At the Melbourne Games, McCormick won the springboard diving easily, beating runner-up Jeanne Stunyo 142.36 to 125.89. The platform diving proved more difficult. With only two dives to go, Pat found herself in second place. She needed two outstanding dives to overtake teammate Paula Jean Myers. Her fifth dive went well, but she remained in second place. Her sixth and last dive, a difficult full twisting 1½, was almost perfect. All she could do was wait. When Myers executed a less than perfect dive, Pat McCormick became the first Olympic diver to win four gold medals.

ANDREA MEAD LAWRENCE

Queen of the Mountain

Andrea Mead Lawrence practically grew up on skis. Her parents were enthusiasts of the sport, and they raised Andrea and her brother in Vermont where "if the weather's good, you ski; if it's bad, you go to school." By the age of six, Andrea had begun her training. "I don't remember getting formal lessons," Lawrence said. "It seemed so simple. We just skied."

By the time she was eleven, she was competing against adults, and at age fourteen, she qualified for the 1947 Olympic trials, where she placed first in the slalom and second in the downhill. She was on her way to St. Moritz.

The 1948 Olympics brought her experience but no medals. Her teammate Gretchen Fraser won the U.S.'s first medal in alpine skiing, a gold in the giant slalom, and took a silver in the combined slalom/downhill.

During the next two years, Lawrence had her share of ups and downs. When the U.S. coach, Friedl Pfeiffer, suggested that she quit racing for a year, Lawrence was horrified. But Friedl had a point; Lawrence had won very few races. "I had been training for skiing night and day since 1947. I was losing the fun of it," Lawrence said. It taught her a lesson. She did not quit racing, but she realized that she couldn't ski well unless she was having fun.

One of the McCormicks' children took up diving. Twenty-eight years after her mother won her second pair of gold medals, Kelly McCormick represented the United States in the springboard competition at the Los Angeles Games. She took the silver medal, finishing just three points shy of the gold; four years later in Seoul, Kelly took the bronze. "She showed me her gold medals when I was a little girl," Kelly said. "I made a bet with her that someday I'd make an Olympic team and win."

Kelly's style was described as "eerily similar" to her mother's. She was graceful and strong, but she lacked the consistency in her dives that characterized her mother's performances.

Kelly McCormick.

Andrea Mead Lawrence at the 1952
Winter Olympics in Oslo.

Gretchen Fraser at the
1948 Winter Olympics in
St. Moritz.

By 1951, Lawrence was having a ball. She was winning many of the races, and her confidence was revived. At the Swiss championships in January 1952, she took second in the slalom and third in the downhill. Team manager Gretchen Fraser, a winner in the 1948 Olympics, was overjoyed. "This is the first time in history that American skiers have made such a showing in international competition," Fraser said. "We'll have a team to reckon with at Oslo."

Fraser was right. When she reached the 1952 Games, Lawrence was ready to attack the slopes and bring home some medals. She won her first event, the giant slalom, by more than 2 seconds, an overwhelming victory in a sport that is usually won by infinitesimal parts of a second. A few days later, Lawrence started the downhill event. At the various checkpoints, she was far in the lead, but she fell inexplicably and was out of contention.

Lawrence was the fifth skier down the slalom course in her last try for another medal. The winner of the event is determined by the combined lowest time of the two runs. On the upper part of the hill, Lawrence had the fastest time of any of the skiers. But in the middle of the course, her ski caught a gate and she overshot it. Luckily, she did not fall. She quickly backtracked and completed the course. Even with the mistake, she was only 1.2 seconds behind the leader. Most people counted her out, but Lawrence had other ideas. Her second run was fast and flawless. She made up for lost time and edged in front by eight-tenths of a second. Lawrence became the first American ever to win two alpine skiing gold medals.

DAWN FRASER

A National Treasure

"I think the ability of Australian women to endure explains a lot of our Olympic success. Women in this country have always been a lot more gutsy than men." —DAWN FRASER

Dawn Fraser won her first gold medal in front of a Melbourne crowd with a world record of 62 seconds flat in the 100-meter freestyle at the age of nineteen. For the next fifteen years, she held the world record in that event and set many other records.

Fraser grew up in a poor working-class family in Sydney. She left school before she was fourteen and spent her time hanging around the pool, where her talent was recognized by swimming coach Harry Gallagher. Most of the time, she trained against men. "I hated the easy assumption that girls had to be slower than boys."

Dawn Fraser at the 1964 Olympic Games in Tokyo.

Fraser became an Australian national treasure, setting twenty-seven individual and twelve team records, becoming the first and only swimmer, male or female, to win the same event in three consecutive Olympic Games. She won more medals (four gold and three silver) than any other Australian in any sport.

Until 1956, Australia had not entered a women's relay team in swimming. Fanny Durack and Mina Wylie had asked to swim the relay in 1912, with each taking two legs of the race, but they were denied permission. When Fraser and her teammates came to the Melbourne Games, they were favored to win. Despite a slow leg by Fraser, who hesitated when she thought she heard a second pistol shot indicating a false start, her teammates picked up the slack and they brought home the gold.

Following her victory in the 1956 Games, Fraser celebrated late into the night. The next day was a free one for her, and she spent the morning exploring Rome. But later that afternoon, she was told that she was to swim the butterfly lap in the medley relay heats. Fraser refused: the butterfly wasn't her event, and she was in no condition to compete.

After the Games, the Australian officials refused to allow Fraser to travel on swimming tours to Japan and South Africa. Fraser's response was to swim better and faster. She broke the one minute mark in the 100-meter freestyle and looked toward future Olympics.

When Fraser joined her teammates at the 1964 Olympics, she was still the fastest swimmer in the 100-meter freestyle. Because her first race was within three days of the opening of the Games, she was forbidden to march in the opening ceremony. Always rebellious and independent, she sneaked into the ceremony anyway. After winning her second Olympic gold medal, she created a stir when she and two men were arrested for climbing a flagpole at the Imperial Palace in Tokyo and removing the flag for a souvenir.

The Australian officials banned Fraser from competition for ten years, ending her swimming career. Although she was reinstated as an amateur four years later, it was too late for Fraser to get into racing shape for the 1968 Olympics. She watched from the stands as her title went to American Jan Henne.

LARISSA LATYNINA

World's First Great Gymnast

The Soviet Union entered Olympic competition in 1952, and the Soviet women gymnasts immediately dominated the new individual sport of women's gymnastics. The most successful of the Soviet gymnasts was Larissa Latynina, who won eighteen medals in the Olympic Games of 1956, 1960, and 1964—eight gold, six silver, and four bronze.

While Latynina remained relatively unknown outside the Soviet Union, she is credited with introducing the art of ballet into gymnastics. A gifted gymnast, she won her medals in the uneven parallel bars, floor exercises, the side horse vault, and the all-around.

Larissa Latynina.

BETTY CUTHBERT

Australia's Golden Girl

When she was eight and living with her family in Ermington, Australia, Betty Cuthbert won the 50-yard and 75-yard sprints at her elementary school. She went on to win the New South Wales combined primary school championships. It was an auspicious beginning for a future Olympian.

June Maston Ferguson, a physical education teacher at Cuthbert's school, was a former Olympic runner. Ferguson liked what she saw in Cuthbert—her natural, flowing style—and persuaded her to join the athletic club she was coaching. Within four years, Cuthbert was entering senior competitions but losing consistently to her clubmate, Marlene Matthews, a powerful

runner who tied a world record for 220 yards. In 1956, Cuthbert's rank was below the world's top fifteen; she had so little confidence that she bought tickets to attend the Olympic Games as a spectator.

Then early in 1956, Cuthbert shocked herself and her coach by breaking the world record in the 200 meters. At the Olympic trials the following month, she won both the 100 and 200 meters. She gave her tickets to her brother John. Betty Cuthbert was going to the Olympics.

Although Marlene Matthews was favored for the 100 meters, Cuthbert won the race easily and took her first gold medal. In the 200 meters, she won again and claimed her second gold medal. Christa Stubnick took the silver and Matthews took the bronze in both races; it was the first time in Olympic history that the medalists in the two sprints finished in identical order. Several days later, she anchored the Australian 4 x 100-meter relay team to victory to win her third gold.

Bets were on that Australia's "Golden Girl" would duplicate her stunning performance four years later in Rome. But a few months before the 1960 Olympics, Cuthbert pulled a hamstring. It acted up in the second round of the 100 meters, and Cuthbert was eliminated. The injury forced her to withdraw from the 200 meters and the 4 x 100-meter relay.

Betty Cuthbert at the 1956 Olympic Games in Melbourne.

Cuthbert retired shortly after. "But then this little voice in my head kept waking me up every night and telling me I should run again," Cuthbert said. "So then I made the decision to try again at the 1964 Tokyo Games and immediately I was able to sleep."

As in 1956, Cuthbert was not the favorite. She'd chosen the 400 meters, a new event for her. In the final heat, she got off quickly and took the lead. When Ann Packer of Great Britain began her push, she cut the distance but not enough. Eight years after winning three gold medals, Betty Cuthbert won a fourth.

WILMA RUDOLPH

"La Gazelle Noire"

The story of African-American track and field star Wilma Rudolph is the quintessence of grace, glory, and the American Dream. Born in 1940 in Bethlehem, Tennessee, the seventeenth of nineteen children, Rudolph's race to the top of her sport started out at a tortoise's crawl.

At age four, she not only could not run, she could not even walk. A case of double pneumonia followed by an attack of scarlet fever had settled in her feet. The pain was excruciating. It was two years of doctor's visits and massages before Rudolph could hop around on one foot, and another two years before she could walk unaided. But by the age of ten, Rudolph was running and jumping and enjoying her favorite sport—basketball.

As a high school freshman, skinny 89-pound Wilma earned the nickname "Skeeter" because her state of perpetual motion reminded her basketball coach of a mosquito. In the summer of her sophomore year, Rudolph ran her first 75-yard dash in national competition and finished fourth. Coach Clinton C. Gray saw a runner in "Skeeter" and recommended her to Ed Temple, the track and field coach at Tennessee State University. Rudolph was off and running.

In 1956, she earned a place on the U.S. Women's Olympic team competing in Melbourne, Australia. The Games did not go well for the American runners. Most of the women, including Rudolph, were eliminated before the finals. The only bright spot was the team's bronze medal in the 4 x 100-meter relay. It was Rudolph's first taste of Olympic glory.

At age seventeen, Rudolph dropped out of track for a year after discovering she was pregnant. But with the support of family and friends, she returned to training on a full athletic schol-

Wilma Rudolph wins the 100-meter race at the 1960 Olympic Games in Rome.

arship at Tennessee State. From there, she blazed the oval running tracks in Amateur Athletic Association (AAU) track and field meets around the country, winning races and shattering records. She had found her "second wind" and looked forward to the 1960 Olympic Games.

Time magazine wrote of Rudolph: "From the moment she first sped down the track in Rome's Olympic Stadium, there was no doubt she was the fastest woman the world had ever seen." Rudolph broke the record for the 100 meters in 11 seconds flat, the first American woman to win a gold medal since 1936. Then she broke the Olympic record in the 200-meter competition and took a second gold. With a flourish, she anchored the 4 x 100-meter relay team for her third gold medal.

Wilma Rudolph became an American icon embraced by people of all races the world over. In her speech later that evening, she pledged to use her physical talents to the "glory of God, the best interests of my nation, and the honor of womanhood."

VERA CASLAVSKA

Escape to Glory

Czechoslovakia's Vera Caslavska won three gold and two silver medals in gymnastics at the 1964 Olympic Games in Tokyo. Four years later, she took a different kind of public stand, signing the manifesto that called for the end of Soviet involvement in Czechoslovakia. When the Soviets sent their tanks into Prague, Caslavska fled to the mountains. There she trained outdoors for the upcoming Mexico City Olympics by swinging on tree limbs and practicing in fields.

Caslavska captured the hearts of people in Mexico and all around the world during the

1968 Games. The crowd adored her; when the judges gave her only 9.6 on the balance beam, they protested with such force that her mark was raised to 9.8. But her greatest show of popularity came during her floor exercises.

The routines of the Russian gymnasts who preceded her were flawless. Caslavska had to do the best floor exercise of her life. The tension was enormous. The room was silent as she stood alone, waiting to begin her routine. When her music, "Mexican Hat Dance," began, there was no doubt about Caslavska's willpower and poise. She showed such grace and acrobatic artistry that she took the gold, adding it to the all-around gold she had already won. She made Olympic history, winning four gold medals and two silvers all together.

Following her competition, Caslavska married teammate Josef Odlozil in a ceremony at the Olympic Village and officially retired from Olympic competition. After the fall of the Communist government in 1989, she was appointed president of the Czechoslovakian National Olympic Committee.

Vera Caslavska on the balance beam.

WYOMIA TYUS

First Winner of Two Straight Olympic Sprint Titles

As a young girl from Griffin, Georgia, Wyomia Tyus's first love was basketball. When basketball season came to an end, Tyus went out for track and field. She first tried high jumping, but she soon realized that the event was not for her and turned her efforts to running.

Tyus was spotted by Tennessee State University coach Ed Temple during a high school track competition in 1961. Temple liked what he saw and encouraged Tyus to participate in his summer training program. After only a month of training, she went to the Amateur Athletic Union (AAU) girls national championships but did not win.

Just one year later, Tyus won the 50-yard, 75-yard, and 100-yard races at the girls nationals in Los Angeles. She broke two American records. In 1963, Tyus continued to excel, finishing second in the AAU women's meet in the 100-yard event. Her good showing led to a trip to Moscow for a United States-Soviet Union competition. Tyus was devastated when she finished fourth in the 100-meter dash against a field of three others. "I wanted to win so bad there . . . All I could remember was finishing last." Two years later, Tyus returned to Russia and tied the world record in the 100-meters, ran second in the 200 meters, and became the world's fastest

Wyomia Tyus runs the 4 x 100-meter relay at the 1968 Olympic Games in Mexico City.

in the 4 x 100-meter relay. Many Americans viewed her commanding performance on national television.

In September of 1963, Tyus entered Tennessee State University on a track scholarship. She became one of the famous "Tigerbelles," twenty-nine of whom represented the United States in Olympic Games from 1956 through 1972. After winning the 100-meter dash in the 1964 AAU women's nationals, Tyus tried out for a place on the 1964 Olympic team. She was so intent upon going to the Olympics that her nerves got to her; she placed third by inches, just making the team.

At the Tokyo Games, Tyus won her heat of the 100-meter dash in 11.3 seconds, the quarter finals in 11.2, and the semifinals in 11.3. She flew by the other runners in the finals and won the gold by two yards in 11.4 seconds.

Four years later in Mexico City, Tyus defended her title by defeating four others who had at some time held the world record. She became the first person in history to win two straight Olympic sprint titles.

THE 1964 JAPANESE VOLLEYBALL TEAM

Never Seriously Challenged

Ten of the twelve members of the Japanese women's volleyball team at the first Olympic tournament in 1964 worked at the same spinning mill in Kaizuku, near Osaka. Their coach, Hirofumi Daimatsu, was a manager at the mill. His training methods were notorious: hitting the young women on the head, kicking them on their hips, insulting them, goading them, making them practice a minimum of six hours a day, seven days a week, fifty-one weeks a year. Daimatsu was the first coach to introduce the rolling receive, in which a player dives to the ground, hits the ball, rolls over, and returns quickly to her feet.

It was befitting that Tokyo would host the first Olympic volleyball event. Japanese sports fans looked forward to the first Olympic volleyball tournament and were the sport's most enthusiastic promoters. Japanese hopes were almost dashed when the North Korean team withdrew over a political dispute, leaving the competition one team short of the six required to conduct an official tournament. The problem was solved when the Japanese helped the South Korean Olympic Committee fund a team.

The Japanese women's team of 1964 was never seriously challenged. They lost only one set, when Coach Daimatsu pulled some of his better players. Eighty percent of Japan's television audience that day watched the competition as the Japanese women won the gold medal.

After the game, the team captain, Masae Kasai, was invited to the official residence of Japan's prime minister, who introduced her to the man she eventually married. Coach Daimatsu retired and, in 1968, ran successfully for a spot in the House of Councilors. He died of a heart attack in 1978.

The Japanese women's volleyball team remained strong, taking the silver medal in the 1972 Games, the gold in 1976, and the bronze in 1984.

The Japanese volleyball team vs. Korea at the 1976 Olympic Games in Montreal.

January 1971 **Coco Chanel dies** January 1972 **Irina Rodnina of the Soviet Union wins her first of three pairs skating gold medals in Sapporo, Japan** August 1972 **Soviet Olga Korbut introduces a more acrobatic style to gymnastics at the Munich Games** January 1976 **In Innsbruck, Austria, Dorothy Hamill wins a gold in figure skating** **Hanni Wenzel wins the first medals for Lichtenstein** August 1976 **Basketball, handball, and rowing are introduced for women in Montreal** **Gymnast Nadia Comaneci achieves the first perfect score ever** May 1979 **Margaret Thatcher is the first woman elected British Premier** December 1979 **Mother Theresa awarded the Nobel Prize** January 1980 **Raisa Smetanina begins her winning streak in skiing** August 1980 **Sixty-two nations boycott the 1980 Games in Moscow** **Zimbabwe wins the first women's field hockey gold medal** September 1981 **Sandra Day O'Connor is sworn in as the first female U.S. justice** June 1983 **Sally Ride is the first American woman in space** February 1984 **Katarina Witt wins her first of two figure skating gold medals in Sarajevo** July 1984 **The Los Angeles Games are boycotted by seventeen countries** **Jackie Joyner-Kersee begins her winning streak in track and field** **Joan Benoit wins the first women's Olympic marathon** November 1984 **Geraldine Ferraro is the first woman to run for vice president of the United States** 1986 **Susan Butcher wins her first of four Iditarod victories** February 1988 **In Calgary, American Bonnie Blair begins her dominance over speed skating** **Midori Ito of Japan introduces a more athletic style to figure skating** July 1988 **Tennis reappears at the Summer Games in Seoul** **Crista Rothenberger is the first woman to win medals in both the Summer and Winter Olympics in the same year** November 1989 **The Berlin Wall comes down** December 1991 **The USSR ends** February 1992 **Kristi Yamaguchi is the first Asian-American to win a figure skating gold medal** June 1992 **Lyn St. James is the first woman to race on the IndyCar circuit, with Rookie of the Year honors** July 1992 **Paula Newby-Fraser is the first woman to break the nine-hour barrier in the Ironman Triathlon** **Hassiba Boulmerka of Algeria is the first woman to compete for her country** **Derartu Tulu of Ethiopia becomes the first African woman of color to win an Olympic medal** May 1993 **Julie Krone is the first female jockey to win a Triple Crown race** February 1994 **Lu Chen is the first Chinese figure skater to win a medal** **American skiers win surprise gold medals in downhill skiing**

The women's marathon at the 1988 Olympic Games in Seoul.

FIVE

With Bells On

1972 TO Present Since the early 1970s, Western women have made further progress in attaining economic, social, and political equality. Margaret Thatcher became the first woman prime minister of Great Britain. Sandra Day O'Connor was named the first female Supreme Court justice of the United States. Cosmonaut Valentina Tereshkova rocketed into space in 1963, the first woman to leave the planet. Still fighting centuries-old societal and cultural restrictions, women from emerging countries began to unite through the efforts of many groups, including a series of worldwide conferences sponsored by the United Nations. Olympic athletes such as Nawal El Moutawakil from Morocco, Hassiba Boulmerka from Algeria, and Derartu Tulu from Ethiopia represent this new spirit of sisterhood and progress at the Olympics.

A look at the Games that have been held in Lake Placid, New York, show the changes in women's involvement. In 1932, Lake Placid hosted its first Olympics with only twenty-one women present to compete. The next time the Games were held there, in 1980, 233 women competed. Following the 1984 Olympic Games, one of the stars, Lynette Woodward of the United States gold-medal-winning basketball team, went on to become the first female member of the Harlem Globetrotters. Women athletes were making their mark and being accepted for their athletic prowess.

The popularity of women's sports and the number of women competitors continued to grow. With television coverage linking the world to the Games, it became clear that more women watched the Games than men. Coverage of women's events thus increased and is now comparable to men's. By the 1992 Games, nearly 3,000 women from all over the globe competed. Fifty-six percent of the television viewers were women. They outnumbered male viewers in all sports except ice hockey. Olympic winners like Bonnie Blair, Jackie Joyner-Kersee, Katarina Witt, and Steffi Graf became household names. The public followed their careers in and out of the sports arena.

For women, the struggle for equality in the Olympic Games has been won. Their participation in a complete spectrum of events, their numbers, and their athletic might have at last secured for them a level playing field in which their grace and glory under pressure are valued and respected. The days of ridicule, restriction, and disrespect are fading echoes. Olympic women of the past ran the good race, and the pure spirit of athletic competition has survived and prospered.

OLGA KORBUT

A Russian Sweetheart

Olga Korbut, a seventeen-year-old just under 5 feet, flew into sports watchers' homes and hearts during the 1972 Munich Olympics. A daredevil of a gymnast, she threw herself around the uneven bars and backward off the balance beam in moves that seemed death defying. She singlehandedly turned women's gymnastics from a somewhat athletic ballet to a breathtaking sport that knew no boundaries. "I don't believe it!" said ABC's color commentator Gordon Maddus when Korbut flung herself into space while performing on the bars. "Give her an 11!" She took home three gold medals and a silver.

The Soviet Union was used to winning women's gymnastics, but in America, Korbut was a star. She met President Nixon and toured Disneyland before returning to her family in Minsk, 180 miles from Chernobyl. A Soviet foreign minister later told her she had done more to

improve relations between Russia and the United States than all of the diplomats of the last five years.

But Korbut's spot at the top was short-lived. Although she won a gold medal and a silver medal competing in the 1976 Olympic Games in Montreal, she was eclipsed by Nadia Comaneci of Romania. She had turned the sport into one for "little daredevil girls," but she herself was a young woman of twenty-one. She retired from gymnastics, married Russian folk-rock musician Leonid Bortkevich, and had a son, Richard, in 1979.

Korbut and her family immigrated to Atlanta, Georgia, in 1991, where she began a coaching career and established the Olga Korbut Foundation to raise money for medical supplies, equipment, and training to aid victims of the Chernobyl disaster. Korbut had not seen the video footage from the Munich Games, and she watched it for the first time in the United States. "I am not the pigtailed girl anymore," Korbut said. "But I hold her dear to my heart." Many Americans feel the same way.

Olga Korbut on the balance beam at the 1972 Olympic Games in Munich.

SHANE GOULD

All That Glitters

In her short but brilliant career, Shane Gould held every freestyle world record from 100 meters to 1,500 meters and the 200-meter individual medley. She broke the oldest record in the books when she beat Dawn Fraser's 100-meter world record, which had stood for almost sixteen years.

Born in Brisbane, Queensland, Gould could swim underwater with her eyes closed at the age of three. She started taking professional swimming lessons when she was six, and at age thirteen, she began to train seriously.

Her performance at the 1972 Munich Olympics was extraordinary. She won five Olympic medals, including three gold medals that set world records. No female swimmer had ever won five individual medals. She also took a silver medal in the 800 meters and a bronze in the 100-meter freestyle.

Gould announced her retirement from competitive swimming the following year. She was looking forward to being an "ordinary teenager." Three years after the Olympics, at age eighteen, she married Neil Innes in a freestyle wedding.

Thirteen-year-old Shane Gould poses with her swimming medals.

NADIA COMANECI

A Perfect Moment

Raised in Onesti, Romania, Nadia Comaneci was discovered at age six by coach Bela Karolyi, who recognized her world-class potential. She was whisked away to a gymnastic training school, where she trained eight hours a day, seven days a week, with two hours for classroom lessons. Before she had turned seven, she defeated five-time European champion Lyudmila Tourischeva.

The training continued to pay off. Comaneci made Olympic history at the 1976 Games in Montreal, scoring the first perfect 10 in gymnastics. Comaneci seemed to soar through the air, combining fragility with strength. Her performance was called "biomechanically inconceivable."

In contrast to Korbut, with her gutsy moves and charming smile, Comaneci was serious, almost grave. She took gold medals in the all-around, the uneven bars, combined exercises, and the balance beam. In all, she received seven perfect 10s. When asked by reporters about her plans for retirement, she reminded them that she was only fourteen.

Comaneci competed again in the Moscow Olympics four years later. There were new, younger gymnasts who charmed the world and earned high scores from the judges, but Comaneci still took a gold medal on the balance beam, silver medals in floor exercise and with her team, and a bronze in the combined exercises.

She retired at age nineteen and took a government coaching post, remaining in Communist

Nadia Comaneci on the balance beam at the 1976 Olympic Games in Montreal.

Romania until 1989. That year, she walked through the night to cross the Hungarian border, where a Romanian émigré, Constantin Panait, waited on the other side. He brought her to the United States.

Comaneci began training with American Olympic gymnast Bart Conner's coach. She took a room in his home, performed in a number of exhibitions with Conner, and, five years later, accepted Conner's marriage proposal. Comaneci and Conner have turned Norman, Oklahoma, into a renowned center for gymnastics, where they have more than 1,000 students.

KORNELIA ENDER

Caught Up in Controversy

A robust child, Kornelia Ender was discovered at age six in a preschool swimming class and eventually enrolled in the Chemie Club training center in East Germany. Like other selected athletes in the Soviet bloc countries, Ender lived away from her family and trained daily. At age thirteen, she anchored two East German relay teams for silver medals in the 1972 Olympics and placed second in the 200-meter race. Over the next four years, she set twenty-three world records.

Kornelia Ender after winning the 200-meter freestyle at the 1976 Olympic Games in Montreal.

Until the 1976 Games in Montreal, no woman swimmer from East Germany had won an Olympic gold medal. Then, in 1976, the East German women's team stunned the world by taking gold medals in eleven out of thirteen events and setting eight world records. Kornelia Ender was the team star, winning the 100-meter and 200-meter freestyle, the 100-meter butterfly, and anchoring the winning 4 x 100-meter medley relay team, all in world-record times.

The success of the East German swimmers was not without controversy, but it wasn't until 1991, after the collapse of communist rule in Eastern Europe, that a number of former East

German swim coaches admitted having given anabolic steroids to some, not all, of their swimmers in the 1970s and 1980s.

Ender was never implicated in the situation. Her father, a colonel in the army, was very much against drugs and made his position clear with the team physician. After the 1976 Olympics, Ender retired from competition against the wishes of the head of East German sports, which put her in a sensitive political position. In the years that followed, Ender married twice and had two children. In 1989, she and her husband attempted to emigrate to the West but did not succeed until the fall of the Berlin Wall. Ender and her family settled in the former West Germany, where she practices physiotherapy.

ANITA DeFRANTZ

Dedicated to the Olympics

Anita DeFrantz's athletic career began as a swimmer at age nine. The only girl on the swim team at a local public park in Indianapolis, DeFrantz was horrified when her father told her that she was going to be awarded a medal for being the girl with the highest points. "But, Dad," she cried. "I was the *only* girl on the team. How can I accept this?" Her father pointed out that she had shown up for every meet, given her best, and was always there to help her team. So later that day, DeFrantz proudly accepted her medal.

DeFrantz's swimming career ended abruptly when the volunteer coach left. As a young African-American girl, her options for playing sports were limited. She was a student at Connecticut College before DeFrantz, 5 feet 11 inches tall, tried basketball. She had no idea how to play the game but she made the team. In her sophomore year, DeFrantz discovered rowing somewhat by accident. She was walking across campus and saw a man standing in front of a boat. When she asked him about it, he introduced her to rowing and said, "You'd be perfect for it." DeFrantz fell in love with what she calls "the noblest of sports. In rowing, everyone is part of the effort."

DeFrantz graduated from college with the dual goals of attending law school at the University of Pennsylvania and making the Olympic rowing team. She trained at the Vesper Boat Club, one of only two clubs in the United States that train women for Olympic level competition.

Before the reunification of Germany in 1990, many athletes from Soviet bloc countries refined their athletic skills under strenuous and highly scientific training methods developed by Eastern European coaches. In communist countries, such as East Germany, children who showed athletic promise often left their families to participate in training programs that controlled their activities around the clock, balancing athletic training with schoolwork.

The emphasis placed on sports and science produced some of the most advanced training methods in the world. Techniques that included a full range of physiological testing were often successful in helping athletes gain an edge over their competition.

Successful athletes and their families often received elite treatment from their governments, including superior housing and access to material goods. In return, they represented their country in a favorable light and provided displays of excellence and skill that generated pride and delight.

In 1976, DeFrantz made the Olympic rowing team and won a bronze medal. The boycott of the 1980 Games dashed her hopes for a repeat performance. However, DeFrantz's participation in the Olympic Movement was not over. She turned her skills toward administration, and in 1986, she became the first African-American woman to serve as a member of the International Olympic Committee. In 1993, she was voted to the executive board.

DeFrantz is also the president of the Amateur Athletic Foundation, dedicated to spreading the ideals of the Olympic Movement to young people in the United States through grants and sports programs. Her perspective: "Sport is a powerful tool that our society needs to understand better and utilize better."

Anita DeFrantz in Los Angeles, 1987.

MARGARET MURDOCK

Sharp Shooter

Some Olympic sports started out as "open" competitions, in which men and women competed together, and were subsequently segregated when separate events were created for women.

When Madge Syers took a second place in the figure skating world championships in 1902, officials barred women and set up a separate competition. Shooting was an open sport until 1984, when events were included for "women only." Yachting was an open sport from the earliest Games, and a number of women won gold medals as crew members. In 1988, women were given their own event for the first time—in the 470 class, a boat in which women are particularly competitive.

In the most recent *Olympic Factbook*, there are thirty-one sports covered for the Summer Games. Six are for men only, two are for women only, one is open, three more have some open events, and the rest have separate events for men and women.

The small-bore rifle competition is not one that draws huge crowds or lengthy television coverage. But the event at the 1976 Games in Montreal closed with one of the most dramatic finals that year.

Favored in the competition was Lanny Bassham of the United States, a silver medalist in the 1972 Games. Bassham's main competitor was teammate Margaret Murdock, thirty-three years old, a mother and a senior nursing student.

Shooting was an open event at that time, and Murdock was the first woman to become a member of a United States Olympic shooting team. One of the few women able to compete on equal footing with the men, Murdock was ranked in the world's top ten greatest shooters by the International Shooting Union. She won seven individual world championships, fourteen world team championships, and five Pan-American gold medals.

The small-bore rifle competition involves shooting at a target from prone, standing, and kneeling positions. After the last rounds, Murdock's name was first on the scoreboard. She had one more point than Lanny Bassham and seemed to have won the gold medal. After an animated discussion, the officials announced that a clerical error had been made in the final tally. One of the judges had written a 9 that should have been a 10 on Bassham's score, leaving

Margaret Murdock and Lanny Bassham share the podium at the 1976 Olympic Games in Montreal.

Bassham and Murdock tied for the gold medal. By federation rules, Bassham received the gold medal because his score included one more 10 than Murdock's.

Bassham was not happy with the decision. Standing on the top step of the victory platform just before "The Star Spangled Banner" began, he reached down and took Murdock's hand, insisting that she join him at the top. Murdock accepted, and together they shared the highest step. "I wanted to show that I felt her performance equaled mine," Bassham said. "There was no way she deserved to stand lower while the anthem was played."

JOAN BENOIT

Marathon Woman

The 1984 Games in Los Angeles marked a true victory for Olympic women. For the first time in Olympic history, women were allowed to compete in the 26.2-mile marathon. The historic occasion reflected the power and determination women have demonstrated in their long, hard battle to be accepted as runners.

As the gun sounded, Joan Benoit of Cape Elizabeth, Maine, took off with the rest of the crowd. At about six miles, she had a lead of 11 seconds over a field that included eleven of the fastest women ever. Nine miles into the race, she was more than a minute ahead. Everyone had expected Benoit to set the pace, but to take such a large lead so early went against accepted marathon strategy. The other runners expected her to fall back to the pack, but Benoit never slowed down. She had had arthroscopic knee surgery just eleven weeks before, but it did not seem to matter. She was in complete control, running her race and nobody else's. Even beyond the halfway mark, Benoit increased her lead. She entered Los Angeles Coliseum to a standing ovation and finished in 2:24:52. With a determined ease, Benoit had shown the world once and for all that women were made to run marathons. "I was so charged up that when I broke the tape, I could have turned around and run another twenty-six miles."

In *Runner's World* magazine, Joe Henderson wrote, "Her win in the first Olympic Marathon for women sealed her spot in history." She held the course record for the Boston Marathon from 1983 until 1994 and as of this writing she continues to hold the American record of 2:21:21.

Joan Benoit wins the marathon at the
1984 Olympic Games in Los Angeles.

JACKIE JOYNER-KERSEE

First Lady of Track

Jackie Joyner-Kersee grew up in East St. Louis, Missouri, where she lived with her parents, a brother, and two sisters in a small house. There was no heat, little money for food, and the neighborhood was infested by gangs and drugs. Joyner's parents kept a strict household with an emphasis on a good education and the independence it brings. Her grandmother named her Jacqueline after First Lady Jacqueline Kennedy. "Some day," she said, "this girl will be the first lady of something."

When she was nine, Joyner joined a track team sponsored by a community center. In her first big race, she finished last. "I didn't have to win," she said. "I just wanted to get better." Then she watched the 1976 Summer Olympics on television and became a big fan of American sprinter Evelyn Ashford. Joyner threw herself into athletics and school with a passion. In addition to running track, she played basketball and volleyball. She competed in the five track and field events of the pentathlon in the Junior Olympics and was named national champion in her age group four years in a row.

In 1980, at age eighteen, Joyner was invited to the Olympic trials, where she finished fourth. Disappointed but determined, she came back four years later and made the 1984 Olympic team. At the Games, she competed in the heptathlon, a grueling two-day competition in seven different events, and missed taking the gold medal by a scant .33 seconds.

Joyner married her coach, Bob Kersee, in 1986, and then went on to set a world record in the heptathlon at the Goodwill Games in Moscow. She broke that record in the 1988 Olympic trials and then broke it again to take the gold medal in the 1988 Games in Seoul. Her crowning achievement

Jackie Joyner-Kersee competes in the heptathlon at the 1992 Olympic Games in Barcelona.

was winning the long jump with an Olympic record of 7.40 meters. "The long jump is my favorite event," Joyner-Kersee said, "because I became a jumper by accident. The coach was waiting for another girl to jump, and I just ran over and leapt."

She repeated her gold medal win in the heptathlon in Barcelona in 1992 and won a bronze in the long jump.

Jackie Joyner-Kersee long jumps at the 1988 Olympic Games in Seoul.

When she retires from sports, Joyner-Kersee—a firm believer in determination, desire, and dedication—plans to pursue a career as a sportscaster while continuing her work with inner city youths. "Women in sports now receive equal recognition," Joyner-Kersee said. "But they still have to work twice as hard as men to be recognized."

FLORENCE GRIFFITH JOYNER

The World's Fastest Woman

She grew up in poverty, the seventh of eleven children. There were days when they ate oatmeal for breakfast, lunch, and dinner. But when Florence Griffith began running as a seven-year-old elementary school student, her life took a different direction.

By the time Griffith graduated from high school in 1978, she had set school records in sprinting and the long jump. She was interested in both business and running, so she enrolled at California State University at Northridge. But money was tight; she could not afford the tuition and had to drop out. Then Griffith caught the eye of Bob Kersee, assistant track coach at California State. He wanted her to continue her academic and athletic careers and helped her get the financial aid to return to college. When Kersee took a coaching position at UCLA, Griffith went too. "My running was starting up," Griffith said, "and I knew Bobby was the best coach for me."

Griffith narrowly missed making the 1980 Olympic team, but she made the 1984 Olympic team and won the silver medal in the 200 meters, just a quarter of a second behind gold medalist Valerie Brisco-Hooks. The defeat knocked the wind out of her sails. By 1986, she was in semiretirement, working at a bank job, writing poetry and children's books, and designing hair and nails. "Running is just something else I do with my life," she said at that time.

However, retiring from running was not in the cards. Early in 1987 she rededicated herself to the sport. She married Al Joyner, a gold medalist in the 1984 Olympic Games, and went to work to improve her starts and speed. Joyner burst onto the running scene at the

Florence Griffith Joyner in the
200-meter race at the 1988 Olympic
Games in Seoul.

76

Olympic trials in 1988, running the four fastest 100 meters in women's track history and taking first place in the 200 meters. She quickly became a media star, with her flashy running outfits, long hair, and painted fingernails. She received offers from film and television producers, modeling agencies, and fashion magazines, glamorizing the image of America's track stars.

Her performance at the Seoul Games in 1988 continued to rewrite the record books. She ran the 100 meters in 10.54 seconds for a gold medal. She went on to break the world record in the 200 meters in 21.34 seconds for another gold medal. Her third gold medal came for running the third leg of the 4 x 100-meter relay. In a surprise move, the U.S. coaches decided that she should anchor the 4 x 400-meter relay team, which she ran just 40 minutes after winning the first relay race. They finished second behind the Soviet Union. "I felt the silver was a special one, because of the team's trust in giving me the chance," Joyner said. "That silver is gold to me."

The spotlight continues to shine on Joyner. Although she announced her retirement from track in 1989, intent upon devoting her time to writing, acting, and business, she will compete again in 1996 in Atlanta.

NAWAL EL MOUTAWAKIL

Breaking with Tradition

El Moutawakil was leading a pack of celebrated hurdlers in the 1984 Los Angeles Games when she jumped the last hurdle and raced toward the finish line. "Deep down in my heart, I was sure I would come in last," she said. But as the tiny Moroccan flew down the homestretch, a vision of her deceased father—who was both mentor and coach—appeared in front of her. She knew she must win. El Moutawakil's time of 54.61 seconds launched her into the history books as the first Moroccan, the first African woman, and the first Islamic woman to win a gold medal. At 2:00 A.M. in her home country, all of Casablanca poured into the streets to celebrate her victory.

Born into the male-dominated, Islamic world of Casablanca, Nawal el Moutawakil had to break traditional rules to participate in sports. Arab women were dissuaded from athletic competition. Before his untimely death, el Moutawakil's father had to accompany her whenever she trained; she could never train alone. "It is very hard for Arab women to do sports," el Moutawakil said. Despite the odds, her father was certain that someday she would become a world champion.

By her late teens, Nawal el Moutawakil was winning gold medals in African and Arab competitions. She attracted the attention of the international track and field community and was offered an athletic scholarship to train and study in the United States. Soon after she arrived, el Moutawakil received word of her father's death. One year later, tragedy struck again. Although she was captain of her college track and field team, el Moutawakil's coach kept her back from a meet to study. The plane carrying her teammates crashed, and everyone was killed.

Nawal el Moutawakil holds the Moroccan flag after her victory at the 1984 Olympic Games in Los Angeles.

El Moutawakil decided to return to Casablanca, intending to give up competitive sports for good. But she stayed long enough to compete for Morocco in the 1984 Games.

Nawal el Moutawakil remains an advocate for Arab women's participation in sport. She coaches the Moroccan Olympic track team and is a journalist for Morocco's *La Gazette du Sport*. In her personal life, Nawal el Moutawakil leads a more traditional Muslim life as a wife and mother of two.

KATARINA WITT

Katarina the Great

Germany's two-time Olympic gold medal figure skating champion, Katarina Witt, donned her first pair of skates at age five after begging her mother for skating lessons. By age ten, she was under the tutelage of East Germany's most famous skating coach, Jutta Muller. Perhaps the first female figure skater to hit the perfect blend of art and athleticism, Witt wowed her audiences with smiles, talent, and sass.

A product of the Eastern European sports system, Witt was supported both financially and professionally through two Olympic Games and four world championships. "If you wanted to be something special in East Germany," Witt told a *Chicago Tribune* reporter, "you did it with sports."

In the 1988 Olympic Games at Calgary, Witt became the first skater since Sonja Henie in 1936 to win back-to-back figure skating gold medals. After the 1988 Games, Witt gave up her amateur status and toured the world skating professionally with American gold medalist Brian Boitano. But she still had the itch to compete. At age twenty-eight, after six years as a professional, she returned to competitive skating and achieved her goal of winning a spot on Germany's reunified Olympic team for the 1994 Games in Lillehammer. "I had a real interesting time this year trying to come back," she said. "I would regret it if I never tried."

Witt knew better than anyone how much women's figure skating had changed in the six years since the 1988 Games. France's Surya Bonaly had a program that included six triple jumps. Oksana Baiul, a sixteen-year-old from the Ukraine, spent so much time in the air that she appeared to float above the ice. Witt respected the newcomers' athletics, but it was not her kind of skating. She did not bring home a third gold medal, but the thrill of returning to the Olympics—and dazzling the audience there one more time—meant more to her than taking a place on the winners stand.

Since the Games in Lillehammer, Witt has returned to professional competition. Her grace and charisma continue to captivate the crowds and win praise from the judges.

Katarina Witt at the 1988 Winter Olympics in Calgary.

79

SYNCHRONIZED SWIMMING

On the Path to Credibility

First added to the Olympics in 1984, synchronized swimming has had to fight for respect. Described as a cross between Esther Williams movies and advanced figure skating, the event has not always been taken seriously. Spectators at the 1992 Games in Barcelona embraced synchronized swimming, and the warm reception perhaps raised respect for the sport.

Competitions were first held in England at the turn of the century. Katherine Curtis, an American swimmer at the University of Wisconsin, is credited with developing the modern version of the sport in the early 1920s, then called water ballet. The sport requires body strength and agility, grace, split-second timing, artistic interpretation, and a lot of underwater swimming.

The phrase "synchronized swimming" was first used by a radio announcer at the 1934 World's Fair. The Amateur Athletic Union first recognized it as a sport in 1945, and it was accepted into the Pan-American Games in the 1950s.

Thirty-four years passed between the demonstration of synchronized swimming at the 1952 Olympic Games and its official debut as a medal sport in 1984. In 1984 and 1992, solo and duet competitions were held. Beginning in 1996, team competition, which is considered the premier event in synchronized swimming, is replacing the solo and duet events. According to Betty Watanabe, executive director of the program commission of the International Olympic Committee, "Synchronizing eight individuals together is what synchronized swimming is all about."

Since the 1984 Games, the United States and Canada have won all eight gold and silver medals, and Japan has taken all four bronze medals. The American team, led by Tracie Ruiz, took the gold medals in 1984. Four years later, Canada won them. The teams switched places again in 1992, when American twins Karen and Sarah Josephson won the duet competition and Kristen Bobb-Sprague took the individual gold medal.

SOUTH KOREAN WOMEN ARCHERS

Straight Shooters

The straight shooters from South Korea became a dominant force in Olympic archery competition at the 1988 Games in Seoul. They swept the women's individual event, winning the gold, silver, and bronze. And the women from South Korea won the gold medal in the newly added team event.

South Korean archers at the 1988 Olympic Games in Seoul.

At the Barcelona Games four years later, the Koreans were shooting well enough to bring home a fistful of medals. The oldest member on the Korean squad, twenty-five-year-old Cho Youn-Jeong, finally upstaged her teammates, Chin-Ho Kim and Soo-Nyung Kim—both gold medalists from the Los Angeles and Seoul shootouts—setting three world records in the preliminary rounds on her way to the first of three gold medals for the South Koreans. Teammate Nyung Kim won the silver in the women's individual behind Youn-Jeong. The Korean shooters then took aim at the team gold, blowing away the Chinese team and claiming the title for the second Olympics in a row.

CHINESE WOMEN'S TABLE TENNIS TEAM

A Long-Standing Dynasty

The women's table tennis teams from China have been in the forefront of international competition for more than four decades. First recognized by the International Olympic Committee in 1977, table tennis was included for the first time at Seoul in 1988. Olympic status has not thrown the Chinese off stride.

Training to become a table tennis champion in China begins at a young age. Potential stars attend a special sports school, where table tennis is the center of their lives. "Table tennis in China takes so much time," said Amy Feng, who placed second in the Chinese National Championships in 1986 before emigrating to the U.S. in 1992. According to Feng, her sports school days began at 6 A.M. with an hour of running and exercise, followed by almost six hours of table tennis, then two hours of studies.

Such rigorous training has kept Chinese women at the top. In 1988, the Chinese women swept the women's singles event, winning the gold, silver, and bronze medals. Teammates Jing Chen and Zhimin Jioo won the silver in the women's doubles.

For the 1992 Olympics, as hundreds of Chinese coaches and players emigrated to the West, China vetoed the appearance of any ex-Chinese who had been living in the West for less than three years. As it

Qiao Hong competes for the Chinese table tennis team at the 1992 Olympic Games in Barcelona.

turned out, China needn't have worried about the women's events. Deng Yaping and Qiao Hong won the women's double for China, upsetting their top-seeded compatriots and the world champions. The women's singles final was an all-Chinese affair with Deng Yaping challenging her teammate Hong. Deng took the first double gold medals in Olympic table tennis.

ROSA MOTA

Portugal's Independent Roadracer

Rosa Mota had not trained specifically for marathon running when she began her long winning streak. Women's distance running had not yet taken off, and Portuguese officials were not supportive. Her coach, Jose Pedrosa, said, "They told me I was foolish to put a little girl in the marathon." However, Mota proved her coach right and marathon officials wrong by winning her first marathon race at the 1982 European Championships in Athens. "At the finish," Mota said, "I was not even tired. Afterward, I went running with my friends from Portugal."

Mota kept on running. She took the bronze medal at the 1984 Games in Los Angeles, becoming the first Portuguese woman ever to win an Olympic medal in track and field.

By the next Olympics, in 1988, Mota was everyone's choice for the gold. She had achieved nine victories in twelve starts, including the 1987 world title in Rome. Portuguese officials continued to give her problems. They were unhappy with her independent spirit and threatened to stop her from competing. In the end, they relented.

Now age thirty, Mota had proven herself to be a marathoner with control. She was able to stand up to pressure and combat the temptation to abandon her racing plan in the throes of competition. The plan she and coach Pedrosa devised for the 1988 Olympic marathon involved surging on a small hill at about twenty-four miles. "I was not worried about Rosa being tired because Rosa never gets tired," Pedrosa said.

Mota made her move exactly as planned and ran the rest of the race alone, running to victory at 2:25:40. To Mota, the time didn't matter. She had run her kind of race. "Medals are more important than times," she said. "Medals stay forever. Times change."

Rosa Mota wins the marathon at the 1988 Olympic Games in Seoul.

Christa Rothenburger at the 1984 Winter Olympics in Sarajevo.

CHRISTA ROTHENBURGER-LUDING

Athlete for All Seasons

Germany's Christa Rothenburger burst onto the Olympic scene in 1984, winning the gold in the 500-meter speed skating event in Sarajevo. The twenty-four-year-old from Dresden won the event in a time of 41.02 seconds.

Eight years before her first Olympic victory, Rothenburger's coach, Ernst Luding (whom she would marry in 1988) persuaded her to take up cycling in the off-season. The idea of cycling terrified her. "I was convinced that as soon as I tried to ride, I would undoubtedly topple right over." Rothenburger got the hang of it very quickly. At her first international competition in 1986—the world championships—she upset Estonian Erika Salumae for the gold medal.

Encouraged by her success, Rothenburger continued to compete in both cycling and speed skating. In 1988, in the Calgary Winter Olympics, she missed the gold in 500-meter speed skating by two one-hundredths of a second behind America's Bonnie Blair, who skated the best race of her life. Three days later, Rothenb·· ne back to win the 1,000-meter race. With a win in cycling at the Seoul Summe· ·me year, she could achieve a gold medal in both winter and summer C·

At the ·mer
Erika Sal·
nipped Roth·
second in the·
Luding took th·
have been fant·
medal," she said,
ble." Nonetheless, ·
became the first athle·
both the winter and su·
in the same year.

Christa Rothenburger-Luding at the 1988 Olympic Games in Seoul.

STEFFI GRAF

The Heart of a Champion

When West German Steffi Graf was four, her father sawed off the end of a tennis racket and moved the couch into the center of the family room where it doubled as a net. If Steffi could return the ball ten times, her father rewarded her with a bread stick. If she could get it back twenty-five times, he threw her a party with ice cream and strawberries.

Peter Graf remained his daughter's one and only coach. "Steffi works much harder than the other girls because she wants to," he told a reporter for *Sports Illustrated*. "That is why she is so good."

At the end of 1984, Steffi was ranked number 22 in the world, but by the end of 1985, she still had not won a tournament. Then things changed. In 1986, Graf had won eight out of the fourteen tournaments she entered. She had defeated longtime champions Martina Navratilova and Chris Evert. She was ranked number 3.

Described as a player with many gifts, including speed and a scorching forehand, Graf overtook Evert for the number 2 spot. She showed a seriousness on the court—the focus necessary for a champion. She loved the game of tennis to the exclusion of any other serious interests, and she had

Steffi Graf at the 1992 Olympic Games in Barcelona.

the heart a champion needs for the long haul. By the end of 1987, she was ranked number 1. In 1988 Graf won the Australian Open, the French Open, Wimbledon, and the U.S. Open, one of five players in history to win the Grand Slam of tennis.

She arrived in Seoul for the 1988 Olympic Games with a five-month, thirty-five-match winning streak. Tennis, which is the oldest Olympic sport for women, was also the newest, reappearing for the first time since 1924. Tennis had been omitted because the early tennis federations felt the sport was not being taken seriously. All that changed in 1988. The Olympic movement was poised to take tennis back with open arms. The game had become both popular and profitable.

Graf faced her most difficult Olympic challenge in the quarterfinals when she trailed Larissa Savchenko 3–1 in the third set. She then won five straight games to close the match. She beat Gabriela Sabatini, the only player to win a match against Graf in 1988, and won the gold medal in straight sets.

In the 1992 Olympics in Barcelona, Graf took the silver medal in singles tennis behind Jennifer Capriati. But Graf has retained her ranking as the top female tennis player in the world. Among her credits are six Wimbledon singles championships. She cherishes her victories even more today, having battled a host of injuries including a bad back in the last two years.

Winners of tennis singles competition at the 1992 Olympic Games in Barcelona (from left) American Jennifer Capriati, Steffi Graf of Germany, and Arantxa Sanchez Vicario of Spain.

STEFFI WALTER-MARTIN

East German Daredevil

Luge is perhaps the most dangerous Olympic sport. Careening downhill at speeds of up to 120 kilometers per hour, the pressure putting the athlete flat on her back can be up to seven times the force of gravity, twice what an astronaut experiences during a shuttle launch. Since its introduction as part of the Olympics in 1964, East Germany has dominated the luge competition.

Steffi Walter-Martin is one of the winners, with gold medals at Sarajevo in 1984 and again at the 1988 Games. She said at the time, "Winning my second is a sweet feeling. I am on top of the world." The ride Walter-Martin took to win her second gold medal was, at best, a rough and challenging one. She took the 1987 season off to have a baby, and her opponents all hoped she'd given up the sport. But she was determined to return to training and get back into shape.

While her husband cared for their son, Walter-Martin began a rigorous training schedule. When the East German Olympic squad was first chosen for 1988, she was the fourth fastest, and there were only three places on the team. Walter-Martin was given a few extra weeks, and she improved her times to qualify for the 1988 Olympics.

The East Germans were not disappointed. Indeed, the East German women swept the event. During five training runs and the competition runs, Walter-Martin and her teammates Bettina Schmidt and Ute Oberhoffner switched places with each other. No competitors from any other countries could break the threesome.

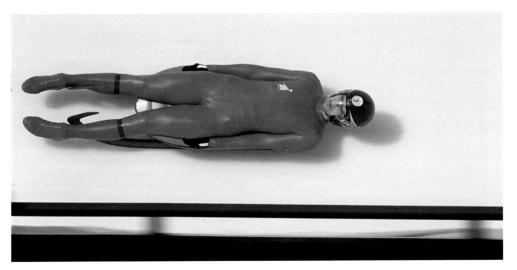

Steffi Walter-Martin at the 1988 Winter Olympics in Calgary.

YAEL ARAD

Israel's First Olympic Medalist

In 1992, Yael Arad became the first Israeli athlete to win an Olympic medal, which she dedicated to the eleven Israeli athletes who were murdered by terrorists at the 1972 Olympics in Munich.

Arad began taking judo lessons with her brother when she was eight years old. She practiced with the boys and won the Israeli championship for her age group when she was ten. At age sixteen, she began to think that she had a chance to be an Olympic competitor. Like all young Israelis, Arad served in the army when she turned eighteen. Following her tour of duty, she continued to train and won a place on the 1992 Olympic team. Four months before the Games, she had an operation on her right knee but she made it to Barcelona. She finished second in the half-middleweight judo competition in a heartbreaking split decision with Catherine Fleury of France. "It was so close, so cruel," she said about the decision.

The Israelis love their first Olympic medalist and cannot get enough of her, demanding interviews and endorsements. "I'm very famous, and sometimes it is too much," Arad said. "But with the publicity I get, I hope that the Jewish children get the message." To encourage more young Jewish people to get involved in sports, Arad started the Yael Arad Foundation for Israeli athletes. "Sport is the purest thing," she said. "When you win in sports, it has nothing to do with politics."

Yael Arad at the 1992 Olympic Games in Barcelona.

DERARTU TULU

Running for Ethiopia

With her victory in the 10,000 meters at the 1992 Barcelona Games, Ethiopia's Derartu Tulu became the first black African woman to win a gold at the Olympic Games. Her victory was an emotional one, as she outran Elana Meyer on the final lap. Meyer was racing for South Africa, represented at the Games for the first time in thirty-two years after being banned for its apartheid policy. With 60,000 spectators cheering wildly, white South African Meyer held

Tulu's arm high and ran the lap of honor. "We both ran for Africa," Meyer said. "I think we did that very well."

Tulu didn't race often in 1992, but she made each race count. Her winning Olympic time was an African record, bettering her own time at the African Games a few weeks earlier, where she won the 3,000 meters and 10,000 meters. Eight weeks after the Olympics, Tulu competed at the World Cup in Havana and became the first woman distance runner to win two events, the 3,000 meter and 10,000 meter titles. She entered only one major road race that year, the Bob Hasan 10K in Jogjarkarta, Indonesia, but she beat one of the most stellar women's fields of the year.

Tulu's 1992 record and her Olympic gold medal brought her the Runner of the Year award.

Elana Meyer (right) and Derartu
Tulu at the 1992 Olympic Games in
Barcelona.

Susi Susanti prepares to serve at the All-England Championships in 1995.

SUSI SUSANTI

Queen of Badminton

It took years of campaigning, particularly by players from Malaysia and Indonesia where it is the national sport, before badminton was introduced in the 1992 Olympic Games. An established sport around the world, badminton is said to be one of the fastest racket sports, with the shuttlecock propelled at speeds up to 200 miles per hour.

Susi Susanti, ranked number 1 in the world, came to the Barcelona Games and won Indonesia's first gold medal in any sport by taking the gold in the women's badminton singles.

Susanti and her fiancé, badminton player Alan Budi Kusuma, delayed their wedding so they could compete in Barcelona. Kusuma beat off all opposition and won the gold in the men's singles event. The two Indonesians were rewarded handsomely by their government after their double gold performance.

Unlike the backyard game that most Americans know, competitive badminton requires great speed, excellent hand-eye coordination, and agility. Spectators at the Barcelona Games filled the newly constructed Pavello de la Mar Bella and greeted the new Olympic sport enthusiastically.

RUSSIAN WOMEN'S BASKETBALL TEAM

Awesome

After staying solidly on top of Olympic basketball since 1976, the Russian women's team placed a disappointing third in the 1988 Games. They looked forward to Barcelona and sweet revenge in 1992.

After the fall of the Soviet Union, the newly formed 1992 Unified Team was strong and experienced, but their semifinal match against the U.S. team proved to be a challenging one. The U.S. women had exploded in the three games leading up to the semifinals, crushing Czechoslovakia, China, and Spain. The Unified Team was the only one standing in the way of the gold medal.

From the start, the Unified Team slowed the pace of the game, running a deliberate offense while sitting back with a zone defense. At halftime, they led 47–41. The Unified Team's coach had a solid strategy for beating the U.S. team's press. The Americans seemed baffled and abandoned the press altogether in the second half after falling behind by 11 points. The U.S. women rallied, and with a little more than five minutes left, the game was tied. The Unified Team surged ahead and won 79–73.

The seesaw battle between the two women's basketball teams continues at the 1996 Atlanta Games. While the Americans are hungry for a chance to prove women's professional basketball, the Unified Team has its pride and reputation at stake. They want to stay on top.

AMERICAN WOMEN'S BASKETBALL TEAM

Now or Never

Despite the fact that American women have been playing basketball since 1891, basketball did not become an Olympic sport until 1976. That year, the American women's team won the silver medal, and they have continued to vie with the Russians for top honors ever since.

The team's Olympic success has not translated into popularity at home. Efforts at major women's professional leagues have flopped, and it was not until 1995, when the University of Connecticut gained national sports attention with its perfect 35–0 season, that the American public begin to embrace the game. Members of the 1996 U.S. team strongly believe that winning a gold medal in Atlanta is the ticket to being treated as professional athletes with a future in professional sports. "It has to be now; it's now or never," said team member Katrina McClain. "This is our chance to get everybody's attention by showing that we can play and it's fun to watch women's basketball."

Nine members of the U.S. women's basketball team have played professional basketball in eight different countries. The lonely nights and huge phone bills take their toll. "It would be awesome to actually be treated as a professional athlete here in America—and have a life, too," said Teresa Edwards, a three-time U.S. Olympic team member who has played professionally in France, Italy, Spain, and Japan.

The U.S. team will crisscross the country three times and tour three continents before the 1996 Olympics. They realize that three weeks of training is not enough. Women's basketball teams from countries like Brazil, the current world champions, are made up of professional players who have frequent chances to play together.

It is definitely a turning point for women's basketball in America. Young girls have embraced the Olympic team, gathering in large numbers wherever they go. "Little girls need big girls to look up to," says Edwards.

The American and Russian basketball teams at the start of a game at the 1992 Olympic Games in Barcelona.

Team sports for women have been slower to gain acceptance at the Olympic Games than individual sports. Field hockey, which was considered the only appropriate team sport for women at the turn of the century, was one of the earliest Olympic team sports for men, first played in 1908. Women's field hockey did not appear at the Games until 1980. The earliest men's team sport was soccer, introduced in 1900. Women will play soccer at the Olympic Games for the first time in 1996. It is a mark of progress that new sports tend to include women from the start. Volleyball, the first team sport for women at the Olympics, was introduced for men at the same time, in 1964. Women continue to seek acceptance in established sports, also. At the 1998 Winter Games in Japan, women will play ice hockey for the first time.

American field hockey team at the 1988 Olympic Games in Seoul.

Women's international ice hockey competition in France, 1908.

HASSIBA BOULMERKA

Running for All Algerian Woman

Hassiba Boulmerka grew up in Constantine, Algeria, 350 miles east of Algiers. As a teenager needing an outlet for her excess energy, she won a foot race in school. Her father did not object to her participation in sports, despite the Muslim belief that women must be covered from head to toe. "My parents supported me all they could," Boulmerka said.

Not everyone in Algeria offered their support. For years, when Boulmerka ran on Algerian roads, men sometimes spat or threw stones to convey their contempt for her activity and dress. Boulmerka persevered. In 1988, she won the 800-meter and 1,500-meter races at the African Games. Later that same year, she represented Algeria at the Seoul Olympic Games. She did not advance past the first round there, but she made plans for the Barcelona Games four years away. She trained four to eight hours a day. "You can't be a champion in a week or a year," she said. "You must accept a time of suffering."

A virtual unknown at the world championships in Tokyo in 1991, Boulmerka won the 1,500-meter race convincingly. She grabbed her hair and screamed "for joy and for shock . . . I was screaming for Algeria's pride and Algeria's history. I screamed finally for every Algerian woman, every Arabic woman." She was the first female world champion from Algeria.

For a time following her world championship, Boulmerka was an Algerian heroine. She and fellow Algerian Noureddine Morceli, who had won the men's 1,500-meter race, were awarded the Medal of Merit, one of Algeria's highest honors. Fundamentalist Muslims denounced Boulmerka for "running with naked legs in front of thousands of men."

Undaunted, she continued to train in Algeria for the Barcelona

Hassiba Boulmerka wins the 1,500-meter final at the 1992 Olympic Games in Barcelona.

95

Games. Once there, Boulmerka ran the 1,500 meters with a winning time of 3:55.30 for her first Olympic gold medal. It was another emotional Olympic moment as she rounded the track in her victory lap shouting, "Algeria, Algeria."

FU MINGXIA

The Face of China

Still a child at the 1992 Barcelona Games, China's Fu Mingxia, age thirteen, was seen in her free time clutching her teddy bear and listening to her Walkman. The rest of the time, she was

diving off platforms ten meters in the air. Her tiny body—5 feet, 93 pounds—would twist and turn in the air and then break the surface of a pool with barely a ripple. By a huge margin of fifty points, Fu Mingxia won the gold medal.

Like all China's divers, Fu was recruited young (age seven) and coached at a training center where training methods are state secrets. She did not know how to swim when she started. Six years later, she took the gold in platform diving at the 1990 Goodwill Games and again a year later at the 1991 world championships.

Fu was born in Hubei province, one of China's poorest areas, and Olympic sport has become her ticket out of poverty. As an Olympic gold medalist, she earned the equivalent of about $3,700, which is the average per capita income over twenty-five years. She and her family enjoy better jobs and housing as a result of her success in diving. And like other Chinese Olympic stars, she wears imported clothing.

Such star treatment, however, has its downside. Her life is supervised closely. Fu and her teammates are expected to concentrate on their sport to the exclusion of an academic education. In a country where intellectual pursuits are prized over physical ones, such one-dimensional training may be an impediment when she retires from diving. For now, she still has a diving career to pursue.

Fu Mingxia prepares to dive at the 1992 Olympic Games in Barcelona.

CHEN LU

China's Ice Princess

China's first figure skating champion, Chen Lu, competed in her first Olympics at Albertville in 1992. She finished in sixth place, an accomplishment for a skater from a country with no figure skating tradition.

When Chen Lu was born in northeast China in 1977, there was no training, coaching, or indoor ice rinks in China. Her father, a former member of the national hockey team, taught her to skate. Isolated from the international world of figure skating, Chen's coach, Li Mingzhu, learned his techniques by watching videos.

By the 1994 Olympic Games in Lillehammer, Chen Lu had gained more experience and exposure. She had what her coach calls *bing gan*, a feeling for skating, and she had expanded her style considerably. Chen Lu won the Olympic bronze medal, showing authority and sensitivity on the ice.

Following her performance at the 1994 Games, Chen Lu continued to rise in international figure skating. She took first place in the 1995 World Championships and silver medals in both Skate America and the Trophee de France later that same year. She has high hopes for winning China's first gold Olympic medal in the 1998 Games.

Chen Lu competes at the 1994 Winter Olympics in Lillehammer.

LYUBOV EGOROVA

Triple Golds

Russian cross-country skier Lyubov Egorova grew up in Tomsk, Siberia, where her parents were defense factory workers. As a young girl, her first love was ballet, but she also excelled at skiing. Encouraged by Soviet sports officials to concentrate on skiing, Egorova moved to St. Petersburg in 1982 to train at the best cross-country course in the country.

At her first Olympic Games in 1992, Egorova medaled in all five races she entered, winning three golds and two silvers. Two years later, in Lillehammer, the twenty-seven-year-old Russian skier was on track to become one of the two most decorated athletes in Winter Olympic history. She skied the last leg of the women's 4 x 5K relay to give Russia a hard-won victory and herself a record-tying sixth gold medal. The only other Winter Olympian with six gold medals is speed skater Lydia Skoblikova who competed for the Soviet Union in 1960 and 1964. She joined Norwegian speed skater Johann Olav Koss as the only triple gold winners of the Lillehammer Games. "It feels good to be the best," Egorova said. "At the same time, it's a victory for the whole Russian team."

So far, Egorova has competed in nine Olympic races in two Olympic Games and medaled in all nine. She plans to compete in the 1998 Nagano Games. At the peak age of thirty-one for cross-country skiers, Egorova has a good chance of winning the most Winter Olympic medals.

**Ljubov Egorova anchors the 4 x 5k
cross-country relay to victory at the
1994 Winter Olympics in Lillehammer.**

BONNIE BLAIR

Speed on Ice

American speed skater Bonnie Blair was born into a skating family as the youngest of six children. She first ventured onto the ice as a toddler, wearing shoes inside the smallest pair of figure skates her mother could find. Some years laters, former Canadian speed skating star Cathy Priestner recognized Blair's potential and talked her into switching from pack-style racing to Olympic-style speed skating. She arranged for Blair to use the University of Illinois rink for practice at six o'clock in the morning. In 1984, an unknown nineteen-year-old, Blair skated to a respectable eighth place in the Sarajevo Winter Games, but she wanted more.

In the 1988 Games, she watched her chief rival, Christa Rothenburger-Luding of East Germany, set a world record. Blair knew she would have to skate the best race of her life. After the 100-meter split, her time was .02 seconds faster than Rothenburger-Luding's. Her first turn "wasn't that good," but her final turn was flawless. Her time of 39.10 seconds translated into a margin of victory of a mere 10.5 inches—about the length of a speed skate blade—in the 500-meter race. Blair had won the gold. She went on to take the bronze medal in the 1,000-meter race and finished fourth in the 1,500-meter race.

Bonnie Blair at the 1992 Winter Olympics in Albertville.

When she returned to compete in the 1992 Games in Albertville, France, the pressure was on. Blair took it in stride and again won the gold in the 500 meters, becoming the first woman to win the event twice and the first American woman to win two consecutive Winter Olympic titles.

In 1994, in Lillehammer, Norway, Blair capped her Olympic career, winning the gold medal in the 500-meter race—making her a triple gold winner in that event and winning the gold for the 1,000-meter race also.

However, Blair was not done. In 1995, she won the women's world sprint speed skating championship, having broken her own 500-meter world record with an even swifter 38.69 seconds the weekend before. "I was hoping I could go a little faster," she said. "But, hey, I'll take it."

The day after her thirty-first birthday, Blair skated her final race on the fast track in Calgary, Alberta. One thing was certain. The world of speed skating would definitely miss Bonnie Blair.

PHOTO CREDITS